WRITING ON THE WALL

An international writing project for Hadrian's Wall 2001-2006

Edited by Steve Chettle ARTS UK

Editorial Consultants Flambard Press

First published in Great Britain in 2006 by ARTS UK
Newburn Enterprise Centre, High Street, Newburn
Newcastle upon Tyne NE15 8LN
Book design and typesetting by GDA, Northumberland
Printed in England by Statex Colour Print, Newcastle upon Tyne

ISBN: 0-9553137-0-8
         978-0-9553137-0-7

Photographers' Credits

The project was photographed over five years and involved a number of photographers. To avoid repeating photographers' names, many of the images carry initials. No name or initial has been shown if the photographer has not wanted to be credited.

Susie Burton	(SB)	Angela Locke	(AL)
Steve Chettle	(SC)	Sara Lurati	(SL)
Stewart Firth	(SF)	Kate Still	(KS)
Morven Gregor	(MG)		

Contents

Introduction

The idea for Writing on the Wall began eleven years ago when two pieces of knowledge collided in my brain to form a concept. The first, a memory of W. H. Auden's 'Roman Wall Blues' read years before by a friend, and the second, a then recent media report on the Vindolanda Tablets, that wonderful collection of military and civilian letters, messages and lists which transformed history into a living, contemporary experience.

Writing on the Wall started in 2001, after major support by Hadrian's Wall Tourism Partnership and significant funding from One NorthEast and other partners.

The core concept has been to commission living writers from the areas most connected to the Wall's line – Tyne and Wear, Northumberland, Cumbria and Scotland, plus the 23 countries in Europe, the Middle-East and North Africa which supplied the original troops and auxiliaries. As a result the project has achieved a natural historical and contemporary internationalism.

Writers also undertook workshops and readings to create an accessible education and participation programme which actively encouraged involvement amongst the people who live along the Wall's line today.

This book results from five years' work by writers who have studied and responded to the line of Hadrian's Wall, its context and content in either historical or modern references or both. This has created a diverse collection of new writing. Human relations, theme parks, tourism, issues of racism, inner city living, love potions, Roman herb lore, archaeology, radio reception through the Tyne Tunnel, the image of the landscape and museum collections are some of the many subjects explored.

Sean O'Brien, Lindsay Allason-Jones and Margaret Lewis, through their essays, provide a clear and comprehensive picture of Writing on the Wall and where it fits into the broader literary setting.

Thanks then go to Jane Brantom and Simon Brooks for their advice and support; to Sean, Lindsay and Margaret for their essays; all the people, groups and organisations who have supported the project or took part in or helped organise workshops and readings; and a special thanks to each of the commissioned writers who between them have created an important new collection of writings about an ancient and modern World Heritage Site – AD 122 to 2006.

Steve Chettle
Director, ARTS UK

For the full set of writings, including those which are only extracts in this book, and more information about the project please go to
www.writingonthewall.uk.com

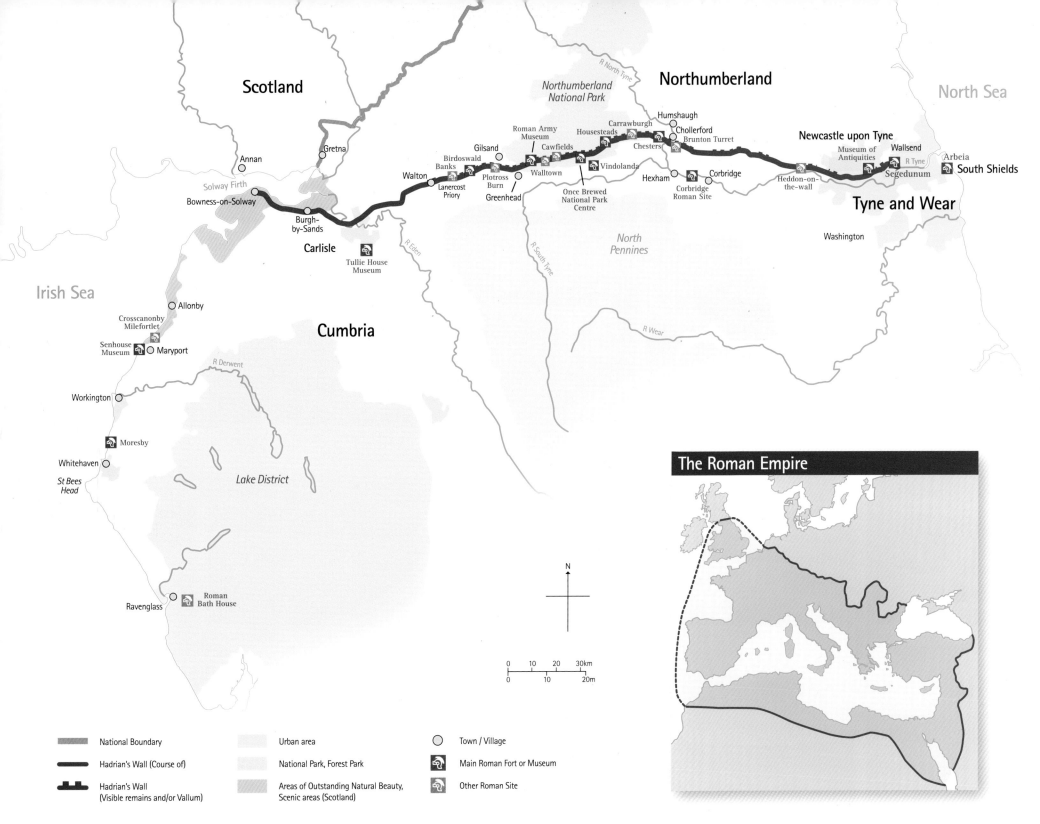

Scotland

Northumberland

North Sea

Northumberland National Park

Annan

Gretna

Humshaugh

Carrawburgh

Chollerford

Newcastle upon Tyne

Roman Army Museum

Housesteads

Brunton Turret

Wallsend

Gilsand

Cawfields

Chesters

Museum of Antiquities

Arbeia

Birdoswald

Walton

Banks

Walltown

Vindolanda

Segedunum

South Shields

Bowness-on-Solway

Plotross Burn

Lanercost Priory

Once Brewed National Park Centre

Hexham

Corbridge

Heddon-on-the-wall

Burgh-by-Sands

Greenhead

Corbridge Roman Site

Tyne and Wear

Carlisle

R Eden

R North Tyne

R Tyne

Washington

Tullie House Museum

R South Tyne

North Pennines

Irish Sea

Allonby

Cumbria

R Wear

Crosscanonby Milefortlet

Senhouse Museum

Maryport

R Derwent

Workington

Moresby

Whitehaven

St Bees Head

Lake District

N

Ravenglass

Roman Bath House

0   10   20   30km

0   10   20m

The Roman Empire

National Boundary

Urban area

Town / Village

Hadrian's Wall (Course of)

National Park, Forest Park

Main Roman Fort or Museum

Hadrian's Wall (Visible remains and/or Vallum)

Areas of Outstanding Natural Beauty, Scenic areas (Scotland)

Other Roman Site

Images which show the urban and rural landscapes through which the line of Hadrian's Wall runs, with Arbeia in the east and finishing with Ravenglass in the west. →

→ Arbeia

→ Arbeia

→ River Tyne

→ Segedunum

→ Westgate Road

→ Benwell Temple

→ West Road fragment

→ Hexham Road, Throckley

→ Heddon-on-the-Wall

→ Chesters

→ Black Carts

→ Limestone Corner

→ View from Sewingshields Crags (SL)

→ Housesteads

→ Birdoswald

→ Carlisle

→ Kirkandrews-on-Eden

→ Solway Plain

→ Drumburgh

All pictures by Steve Chettle, except view from Sewingshields Crags

→ *Wallsend*

→ *Byker*

→ *Ouseburn*

→ *Pons Aelius*

→ *Newcastle looking west*

→ *Eppies Hill*

→ *Harlow Hill*

→ *East Wallhouses*

→ *Vallum, Wall Houses*

→ *Corbridge Roman Fort*

→ *Vindolanda*

→ *Milecastle 42*

→ *Walltown Crags*

→ *Walltown Quarry*

→ *Gilsland*

→ *Bowness-on-Solway*

→ *Mawbray*

→ *Maryport*

→ *Moresby*

→ *Ravenglass Bathhouse*

Research →

Workshops →

(AL)

(AL)

Readings →

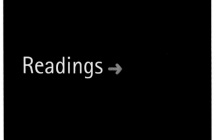  

All pictures by Steve Chettle, except where indicated.

Photo: Caroline Forbes

Sean O'Brien

Sean O'Brien is a poet, critic, playwright and
editor. Five award-winning collections, most
recently *Downriver* (2001), which won the
Forward Prize, were followed by *Cousin Coat:
Selected Poems* 1976–2001 (Picador, 2002).
His essays, *The Deregulated Muse* (Bloodaxe),
and an anthology, *The Firebox: Poetry in
Britain and Ireland after 1945* (Picador),
appeared in 1998. His plays are published
by Methuen and his short stories by Comma
Press. He is Professor of Poetry at Sheffield
Hallam and a Visiting Professor at the
University of Newcastle upon Tyne. His version
of Dante's *Inferno* will be published by Picador
in October 2006 and a new collection in 2007.

Writing on the Writing on the Wall

Instead of being responses to the inherent significance of rivers and mountains, forests and oceans, and to those man-made sites which compel the imagination, nowadays the meanings which humankind has always discovered in the environment are often said to be our own inventions. Yet though the world has allegedly undergone a disenchantment, we are still magnetized to certain locations. Their resonance is specific and non-transferable: hence we go back to them or, with luck, we live alongside them. Many people have personal lists of such sites. Mine would include Venice, Red Square and New Orleans, and Hadrian's Wall is likewise an eminent example of a place that continues to seem charged with meaning.

It is of course stretching a point to describe the Wall as 'a place' in itself. It is extensive and multiple, gapped but imaginatively continuous. It links the coasts, serves as an ancient political division, raises a rampart against marauding Picts and has offered a source of building-stone for farmers indifferent to the big picture. It also provides a giant time-piece by which to measure the evanescence of human life – a condition which the Wall, like all great monuments, renders both melancholy and strangely satisfying to contemplate. 'Look on my works ye mighty and despair!' writes Shelley in the intensely pleasurable 'Ozymandias'. The Wall might be called a world in its own right. It presents one of the richest metaphors of our infinitely various condition. It is capacious, mysterious, hospitable to multiple and contradictory interpretations, as much at home to the individual – the Roman legionary, the Victorian antiquary, the present-day walker – as to the imperial strategy which ordered the vast and ingenious labour which went into its construction.

← *View from Sewingshields Crags*
Photo: Sara Lurati/ARTS UK

Given the immense imaginative resource provided by the Wall, it is surprising that a project such as Writing on the Wall has not been undertaken before. In fact, though, the project demonstrates the meeting of two important strands in contemporary thinking about writing: firstly that writers – poets, most often – should be enlisted in public projects, and secondly that the participation of professional writers should be matched by broad public participation, across the range of age and ability. This is of course by no means the first time such work has been done – it has become a staple of arts activity – but it seems especially apt to the Wall, where people of all kinds, often drawn from remote places – the Roman army itself recruited as far afield as North Africa, Romania and Turkey – have wandered, fought, loved and worked during two thousand years. It is in a real sense public property, a site in which everyone – including many who have yet to visit it – can be said to have a stake. The work of Writing on the Wall has been firmly planted on the Wall itself, in dramatic performances, readings, workshops, talks and – most welcome – in international encounters between writers and audiences.

In its cunning way, W. H. Auden's 'Roman Wall Blues' takes account of this wide ownership. Auden balances comedy with the exasperated gloom of the Roman legionary who actually has to live those rigours – cold, dirt, frustration, jealousy, boredom – which the poet is free to imagine from the comfort of his study. The poem thus offers a humanizing balance to imperial grandeur. Indeed, the soldier's preoccupations lend reality to the grand abstractions he must glumly serve. Linda France's 'The Love Potion of Polemios', derived from an engraved ring found at Corbridge, explores another aspect of the private sphere, the erotic, which for a time overrides the claims of the political world while exploiting its language: 'He looks at me / slowly and I glisten. Makes me wait / till the sun is an arrow in the sky. / The best omen. He is the Emperor / of Amber…'

This theme of doubleness takes another form in W.N. Herbert's work, which is fascinated by the way in which the Wall both joins and divides, and by how it defines the space which will in time overcome it: 'here begins beyond'. Herbert's ballad, 'Song of the Marchmen', investigates what Auden's legionary ignores – who 'we' are, who 'they' are, and what we're doing here. These are questions of enduring relevance, whether on the scale of neighbourly grousing, or in the eruption of civil war, when the vanity of empire exceeds its power to understand or control the consequences of its folly. Katrina Porteous' 'The Ruined Thistles' exemplifies the permanence of such themes, and the contradictory 'truths' which they offer. Porteous recalls Ted Hughes' fine poem, 'Thistles', but where Hughes writes in praise of persistence and courage, Porteous sees the thistles' persistence as evidence of inescapable folly: 'Their wits fly away like smoke / Into next year, and the next.'

There is, quite properly, no single appropriate summary for the work undertaken by Writing on the Wall. It offers a rich and diverse mixture of writing at all levels from the expert to the novice. It exemplifies and celebrates co-operation and exchange of skills and ideas. It affirms the arts of peace, on a site intended to enshrine conflict. It draws the imagination back to the familiar strangeness of the Wall itself. It commends the examined life, which is all the justification anyone can require. Hafsa Bekri-Lamrani imagines the shade of the Emperor Hadrian in the King's Arms declaring: 'Poets and poetry taught me / History's ephemeral vanity / and the strength of life over stones'. We live in hope.

Photo: Glyn Goodrick

Lindsay Allason-Jones

Lindsay Allason-Jones is Director of
Archaeological Museums for the University
of Newcastle upon Tyne and Reader in
Roman Material Culture. Her main research
interests lie in the lives of the people of
the Roman Empire, using inscriptions and
artefacts as evidence. She has written
nine books (including one novel) and over
100 papers on topics relating to Romans
and natives in Britain and the Empire.

Tombstone of Regina, who died at South Shields
Photo: Museum of Antiquities of the University
and Society of Antiquaries of Newcastle upon Tyne

Ancient Words

The Roman period is the first in Britain when we know that a written language was in use. It is through this written medium, whether it survives on wax tablets, wooden sheets, lead curses or stone slabs, that we know as much as we do about life in the province of Britannia. The bulk of these inscriptions are in Latin but some are in Greek, the language of the truly educated Roman, whilst others, such as Barates' memorial to his Romano-British wife Regina in his native Palmyrene script, represent the cosmopolitan nature of Britain at the time.

Leaving inscriptions on stone tends to be a military habit throughout the Roman Empire so it is not surprising that the north of England has the majority of the inscriptions in stone that have survived in the province. Some of these inscriptions are formal records of activities, such as the tablet from the River Tyne at Newcastle marking the safe arrival of vexillations from the three legions responsible for building the Wall or the important inscription from Jarrow that tells us that 'after the barbarians had been dispersed and the province of Britain had been recovered, he [Hadrian] added a frontier line between either shore of the Ocean for 80 miles'. Others are more personal, like the tombstones that record the lives of a range of people: men, women and children, soldiers and civilians, the free, the freed and slaves. The relationship between these people and their gods is also known through altars, some very small and dedicated by one person, some very large and dedicated by a unit. Through the building stones, altars and tombstones we are privileged to be introduced to individual people by their names, often with details of their origins, families and status.

The Wall itself was inscribed with centurial stones – short texts that give the name of the century responsible for building a particular stretch of curtain wall or a specific milecastle or fort building. These may have had a dual purpose, both a method of quality control allowing the authorities to check on the centuries' building standards, and as a bonding mechanism, a marking of a community project successfully achieved by a small body of men working together.

Occasionally an inscription shows how people could use their literacy and education to further their own ends. From Carvoran, for example, we have a startling exercise in sycophancy as Marcus Caeciluis Donatianus leaves a poem linking the Emperor Septimus Severus' wife, Julia Domna, with the goddess Virgo Caelestis following a vision. Cynically, we can only presume that the vision was of a successful career should the Emperor see the poem during his visit to Britain, rather than a truly religious experience.

To the Roman army literacy was essential for the smooth running of the Empire. The sheer distances involved required an efficient method of communication. The Emperor needed to be kept informed about each province so that each level of military or civilian government could be controlled and their activities recorded. So important was literacy that a soldier could not gain promotion to centurion unless he was able to read and write. The fact that the Romans liked to keep records in quadruplicate is a reminder of how easy it is for the desire to communicate to develop into bureaucracy.

The exciting discovery of many wooden writing tablets at Vindolanda has allowed us to learn about the Roman mania for keeping lists, whether lists of supplies, men or festivals. Some link all three as they record the foodstuffs required for religious festivals as well as the suppliers of the chickens, beer, wine, suckling pigs, radishes and venison needed for the holiday feasts, with an indication of how much each commodity cost. The tablets have also given us a glimpse into the more personal lives of the military community in the area as several letters have survived, some between friends, some more officially asking for favours from a commanding officer. Amongst the former, the correspondence between Aelius Brocchus and his wife Lepidina and their friends Flavius Cerialis and his wife Claudia Severa, which includes the famous birthday party invitation, offers an insight into the lives of officers and their families on a far-flung Roman frontier. It is these personal glimpses and occasional references that we can all relate to, such as the complaints by Octavius about the poor roads around Catterick which are interfering with his supply route, resulting in his financial embarrassment. These reveal the differences and similarities between life in the area in the Roman period and our lives today – details that pure archaeology can rarely provide.

Letter from Octavius to Candidus
© *The Vindolanda Trust*

Margaret Lewis

Margaret Lewis, who was born in Northern Ireland and grew up in Canada, first visited Hadrian's Wall in the 1960s and was captivated by the scent of heather and the sound of curlews. Her career has spanned teaching and administration for the Universities of Durham, Newcastle upon Tyne and the Open University. She has published biographies of crime novelists Ngaio Marsh and Ellis Peters, and, most recently, of the sculptor Josefina de Vasconcellos. With her husband Peter Lewis she lives very near the Mithraeum at Carrawbrough and jointly edits Flambard Press.

Who Owns the Stones?

Poetry can take you by surprise. A poet can set an ambush; can extract responses that are unexpected for the writer and the participant. Both can find rewards. This interaction between the writer and the public was a central part of an ARTS UK concept which began in 2001. Northern writers joined with an international group representing some of the far-flung peoples of the Roman Empire who built and garrisoned the Wall. Poets from Morocco, Romania, Iraq, the Netherlands and Bulgaria visited the Wall and responded to it. They were maintaining a long tradition, because writing has always been part of life along the Wall, as Lindsay Allason-Jones shows us in her fascinating introduction.

Individual poets reflect history in a multitude of ways and bring contemporary concerns to bear. Some found it easy to imagine life among the settlements that lined the military installation itself, especially the life of women and ordinary soldiers. The idea of the Wall as a barrier became significant to several poets, and also the lingering sense of a lost empire, withering away. The land beyond the Wall was always present as a defining force. All these poets found that their own work was being enhanced by the interweaving of contemporary issues with a response to landscape and the historical events connected to it.

When Katrina Porteous worked with the farming community near Haltwhistle in 2002 she listened to the concerns of farmers along the Wall who have to work in a World Heritage site. She felt the grief, still poignant, of farmers and their families who had watched while healthy animals were slaughtered during the Foot and Mouth epidemic a year before. Her poem 'Two Countries' with its reference to 'the ungrazed fell' reminds the reader of those unhappy times. Reading her poems in a pub on the Wall, accompanied by a Northumberland piper, was a chance for Katrina to reach out, and for local people to respond.

In contrast to Katrina's individual, questing, approach, Bill Herbert concentrated on inspiring schoolchildren in South Shields and Wallsend. Bill energetically took the youngsters on site visits to Segedunum and Arbeia, and from these came not only poetry but an exciting response to their historical environment. Bill's own thoughts brought him to a renewed sense of space and time as he travelled the length of the Wall, leading him to conclude that 'you start to feel the Romans got the border right'.

Several poets took Roman artefacts held in museums to create a focal point for workshops and discussion. Jacob Polley used the handling boxes of Roman exhibits in Tullie House Museum, Carlisle, as well as written source material with his creative writing group. These voices from the past proved particularly valuable and Jacob found that 'they did not, as I had feared, want to hold too fast to the facts, to the detriment of their own imaginative work'. Not surprisingly, his poem 'History' celebrates the objects of everyday life that survive.

Linda France used a similar approach with a group who visited the museum at Corbridge Roman Fort and were encouraged to think about the artefacts relating to women's lives along the Wall. Her imagination swoops and glides like a skylark in her poem 'The Love Potion of Polemios', which was inspired by an engraving on a ring found at Corbridge.

Farah Begum-Baig notices the minute details in the presence of the Wall in her delicate poetry. A spider's web, a dewdrop, the dome of stars above dark Northumberland are linked to observations on the modern military installations nearby and to the chatter of lively coach parties visiting the Roman ruins.

For Bulgarian born poet Kapka Kassabova it was the inscriptions on tablets and tombstones left behind by the Romans that inspired her to weave a narrative to complete the fragment. Her poems astutely incorporate the actual words also referred to by Lindsay Allason-Jones. We are gripped by Kassabova's sense of the shortness of lives at the time and the vulnerability of Roman women far from home.

The poet and historian Robert Forsythe worked with a school in Heddon-on-the-Wall, and encouraged creative responses to film and to poetry written about the Wall, such as W. H. Auden's famous 'Roman Wall Blues'. He also recorded a trip along the Wall aboard the Hadrian's Wall Bus which goes daily from Wallsend to Bowness-on-Solway, picking up walkers and cyclists along the route. As Robert says, 'there has to be some logic to creating a bus route between Wallsend and Bowness-on-Solway and a clue comes in the route number which is rather strange: AD122'. (This is, of course, the year in which the Emperor Hadrian made his first visit to the British Isles.)

Poets representing the origins of soldiers who had been posted along the Wall visited schools across the region. Iraqi poet Hashem Shafiq found the experience of reading and listening to primary schoolchildren in Newcastle 'a unique and enchanting encounter'. He read in English and Arabic and found that 'those children returned me back to my childhood and brought me close to poetry'.

Archaeologist and writer Esther Jansma read her poems in Dutch at Housesteads, and responded deeply to the sense of history that is inescapable on those high and lonely stretches of the Wall. In her poem 'The Collector' she writes of 'moments long ago,/ which really were and which are really/ vanished till someone grasps them, reads them back'.

Romanian poet Denisa Comanescu found lost lives in the wooden tablets at Vindolanda and made a connection to the record on Trajan's Column in Rome of an early Dacian king, Decebalus, who defeated the Roman Fifth Legion in 87 AD. She sees the people and the relationships behind the inscriptions in 'A Birdoswald Sequence'. In 'Vindolanda: a Utopia' she binds together the idea of the Wall with language and friendship: 'The gates of milecastles are wide open,/The ditch filled with poems'.

Hafsa Bekri-Lamrani, from Morocco, talked to schoolchildren in Bowness-on-Solway and Burgh-by-Sands about words and the different languages that unite and divide us. The youngsters inspired her too: 'Speak with your heart to kids and they will understand!'

Iraqi writer Samuel Shimon evoked his ancestors as he visited the Tyne, and realizes that they were slaves, brought to Roman Britain from Mesopotamia. Shimon's story is full of mixed emotions, of longing and sadness, but the human spirit endures. From his memories comes his short story 'Kika and the Ferryman'.

On the west coast, in Ravenglass, poet and novelist Kitty Fitzgerald was working with the primary school and in the community. She was fascinated by the use of herbs by the Romans, and the evocative scents of flowers and aromatic stems runs through her poems. Her men and women of the Wall are forever alert to the threat from the Celtic tribes beyond.

Angela Locke was also on the west coast, and worked for an extended spell in Maryport. Her writing group, based at Senhouse Roman Fort, has flourished and produced prize-winning poets. In Angela's own poetry, walls as dividers fall into several categories, ancient and modern. She sympathizes with the ageing Centurion who walks the Wall looking to the north, in bitter winds, but thinks longingly of warm springtime to the south, in his home, Hispania.

Penny Grennan, too, was able to step easily into the mind of the weary soldier in the bathhouse, easing his aching frame into warm water after hard service on the Wall. She finds an interesting historical note in 'Stone for St Oswald Head Farm' which describes a practice common for many centuries, when the stones were taken for contemporary buildings. The farmer is a little guilty, but defiantly asks, 'Who do these stones belong to anyway?' A good question, and one that Peter Mortimer developed in his play, *Off the Wall.*

Ellen Phethean's long poem 'Wall' takes in the challenging territory of the Byker Wall in inner-city Newcastle upon Tyne. She creates a poetic narrative involving many characters and tells the story of their lives. Racial tensions, drugs, teenage pregnancies, poverty and loneliness all weave their way into this epic poem. But there is life in abundance, and love as well. There are even a few relics of the earlier Roman Wall. The extracts published here give only a taste of a rich feast contained in her book.

Dramatist Alex Ferguson also addresses racial sensitivities in his short story, *A Place of Honour.* He explores the irony of contemporary immigrants from the Middle East, resented locally, finding evidence of their forefathers carved into ancient stones in a Roman fort. History would inform the present, if prejudice allowed.

Writing on the Wall has been stylishly displayed on the World Wide Web, where people in many countries can share in what was already a wide-ranging experience. This publication will bring together some of the fine writing that the project has inspired. Like all good ideas, Writing on the Wall should continue over time to reach out and involve others, gathering them round the enduring focus of Hadrian's Wall.

So who does own the stones? Every writer, every artist, every musician, every visitor who has stopped to wonder and to respond to this World Heritage site. This Heritage is for us all.

The Writers

Photo: Robert K S Bower

Farah Begum-Baig

Farah Begum-Baig, who has been writing poetry since she was six, was educated at the University of Newcastle upon Tyne and Trinity Hall, Cambridge. She was involved in medical research and teaching at Cambridge University and contributed to radio, TV and books. Her career has combined medical research, complementary medicine, and scientific and creative writing.

For many years she lived in a cottage on Hadrian's Wall with her sculptor husband, focusing on writing poetry, plays and films. She still lives within sight of the Wall, which remains a tangible presence in her physical and mental landscape.

After the Rain

Wire infiltrates the old beech tree

Between hexagons of twisted metal sags a spider's web
outlined with fine miniscule beads

Where three threads meet the Web drips
heavy rain drops
sparkling rainbows

A pendant single leaf twists clockwise
unravelling

Living by a thread
patient pragmatic spider
continues repairs.

Bliss

A dew drop
glistens on a blade of grass

Simple things
bestow most pleasure

Joy bubbles, suffusing body
Soars out, a blissful smile

Thirst slaked

Oasis in the desert strife of modern life.

Starlight on Hadrian's Wall

Stillness, quiet and dark
the sky's dome hangs
pricked by stars

2000 years ago men from Rome built this
Weathered stones lasting testament
to sweaty energy of men long dead

Did they also look and marvel?
Starlight gleams yellow, blue, white, green
my thoughts spiral, how do they compare with the speed
of light? Some stars so far from earth they no longer exist
yet their light has just reached me

Mesmerised by a brilliant star
an astronomer somewhere will also see and name it
although the star was extinguished long ago
and now is nothing but light.

Chesters Roman Fort

Hadrian's Wall bus
AD 122
halts

spills out tourists
herded by tour guides
grazing the officers' quarters
and communal bath houses

WI members cluck
over well preserved hot water pipes

Kids from year 9
flirt like mad
not interested in museum artefacts
only erotic Roman graffiti.

After

After the Wall has fallen
crumbled to
dust

my body
reclaimed
by soil

my soul
joining
those of
Roman soldiers

becomes one
with The Light glowing in darkness.

Hadrian's Wall World Heritage Site

No terracotta army here
Roman legionnaires long gone

Now explosions at Spadeadam
Those who kill by stealth and
Leave the song of ewes

Laments for their lost lambs
Echoes within a baby Grand Canyon
Cascade down Butterburn's waterfall

No pyramids, no Nile
Sphinx-like
The Wall stands and
Knows I am here.

The Gift

In the womb,
the unborn child
possessor of magic powers

Saviour
Joy to family, friends and all

No time and all time

Tacit

Hope for the future
Healing wounds.

Lucky Dip

My best friend is a murderer
They say every child chooses its parents
I wish her baby had chosen me.

*Inspired by the Vindolanda Tablets, an epitaph
to a baby, and the tombstone of Anicius Ingenuus,
a Roman army doctor, found near Housesteads.*

Hafsa Bekri-Lamrani

Hafsa Bekri-Lamrani was born in Mecheria, Algeria, near the Moroccan border, to parents of Moroccan origin. She graduated from Paris VII University with a master's degree on British Romantic poets and a DEA on the British Industrial World. She is presently working on a PhD on East and West in Shelley's poetry.

She taught English Language and Literature in teacher training colleges in Morocco from 1979 to 2005, and has participated in and co-founded various NGOs in Casablanca, such as The Women and Development Association, The House of Poetry, The Mediterranean Research Centre, and The Al Madina Socio-cultural Association. Her publications include *Jellabiates* (2001), *Berbers in Solway* (internet by ARTS UK) and *Tendresse et autres Lumières/Sparks of Life* (2005).

How to Spell Bowness on the Way to Your Soul

The Wall as an excuse,
People as a very good reason,
Magic landscape as a
Dream place,
Birds as a symphony of Life and
Peace be on you all.

On the Border

Being on the border
On the edge
On the verge
On the brink
On the brim
On the rim
On the fringe
On the coast
On the bank
Of Scotland and
Finding an open door

No boundaries
No barriers
No pillar of Hercules to crush
No Rubicon to cross
Only a few stoned dwarf Wall
In a dreamlike nature
Now veiled in mist
Now blooming in the sun

And

People!
All the Grahams and Bells
The Ogles and the Pringles
The Armstrongs and the Robsons
The Nixons and the Dixons
The Scotts and the Elliotts
The Ridleys and the Beatties

All these and other Reivers
Once dreaded warriors
Now peaceful farmers or
Haafnetters
Joined for ales or else
In King's Arms pub
With no arms but
Darts to play and jokes to share

I felt tempted
In this land
Teeming with ghosts
To ask Hadrian's soul
Perhaps present and invisible
In some corner of this pub
Where his fort once stood,
Ask his two thousand year old soul
About people and barriers.

And I could almost sense
A smile on his face
As he would tell me:
'Poets and poetry taught me
History's ephemeral vanity and
The strength of life over stones
At the self moment I was building
Walls'

And Hadrian's soul
Suddenly vanished
As Lawrence in his Scottish kilt
Gave vent to a cry of joy:
He had won the darts game!

A Piece of Paradise

The sky this morning is under my feet, for the sky here is not hopelessly blue as in my country. Here, it generously rains itself into the ground and grows back velvety green. (The second I finished this line, the sun came out!) Well, I will not take my line back since Scotland across from me has decided to be veiled in misty mystery like a dreamy oriental woman.

Birds around me underline the spiritual depth of silence with their harmonious, colourful songs. I raise my eyes for inspiration and a diamond gently held by crossed weeds shines in the sun. The sun surely wants to play a hide and seek game with me on this spot of the universe. Dew and sun! So many liquid diamonds to treasure with your eyes and keep safe in a secret corner of your memory!

Still spiting me, the sun, now hot on this side of the shore, stretches his arms and indecently tries to unveil Scotland, which resists him like a shy young girl. Insisting still, the many armed ball of fire darts his hot rays through my clothes and forces me to take off my coat. I complain to a green ladybird which ignores me and goes on. I walk back to Bowness, my shadow on my left side and the sun above my head.

Bowness-on-Solway, 4 April, 2002

Bowness-on-Solway looking to Scotland across the Solway Firth →
Photo: Steve Chettle

Photo: Steve Chettle

Denisa Comanescu

Denisa Comanescu, who was born in Buzau, Romania, in 1954, is a poet, editor and translator. She is the author of five volumes of poetry and the recipient of several poetry prizes in Romania. A volume of her selected poems, translated by Dan Shafran, was published by the Swedish publishing house Gondolin in 1999. Her poems have been included in anthologies in fifteen countries. In the UK her poems have appeared in three anthologies, including *When the Tunnels Meet: Contemporary Romanian Poetry* (Bloodaxe, 1996; translated by Eiléan Ní Chuilleanáin).

Vindolanda: A Utopia

My friend writes in a special language:
It's a forgotten and redeemed language
like the wooden tablets of Vindolanda.
She also used to live in our common language;
the border between them not being quite firm
as the ruins of Hadrian's Wall.

By each new written line
the Wall has slowly been moving to the North:
Now you can see no soldiers patrolling its top,
The gates of milecastles are wide open,
The ditch filled with poems.

My friend's language has no more territory to conquer.

A Birdoswald Sequence

A child was named Decebalus.
He was born in AD 205 in the valley of Irthing,
beyond the Roman fort.

His father guarded the Wall –
endlessly patrolling
his ears ready to catch
the slightest sound rushing from the North.
The wind had emptied his mind
so that he could easily have written poems.

His Brigante lover did not know
why their son had got this name,
she was only praying
her Dacian Soldier might neither be moved away
nor be killed by the Picts.

He kept saying
that after ten years he would be freed,
awarded some land, marrying her
and happily living together
just here, beyond the Roman fort.

Their common language was the Wall.

Decebalus *(Braveheart or The Heroic One) refers to the
nickname of the early Dacian King Diurapneus, who defeated
the Roman 5th Legion in 87 AD and who subsequently died
in a later Roman conquest of Dacia in 105 AD.
Many of the events are documented on Trajan's Column.*

Testimony

One hundred cats signed
on the hot tiles of the Roman bath
in Vindolanda,
and only one soldier.
But the sole of his sandal
had a patterned design of gems.

Alex Ferguson

Alex Ferguson was born in Jarrow and still lives on Tyneside. Founding dramatist Corin & Vanessa Redgrave's Moving Theatre; 1997 Writers' Guild Winner Best Radio Comedy/ Light Entertainment; Creator of *My Uncle Freddie*, award-winning radio series; published *The Pineapple King & Other Stories* IRON Press 2004. Creative Director *Bold as Brass* Young People's Theatre Company; C. P. Taylor Bursary Winner 1994; Northern Playwrights Society 1995; Drama Award Winner Plays International; Guinness National Award for Pub Theatre, 1997; Nomination Royal Television Society Regional Award 2004 *Lads!* ; The Pride of Place Festival 2004: *The Stars Look Down.*

A Place of Honour

An excerpt from his short story

'Here on the site of the Roman Fort,' said Miss Bagley, brightly, 'the West Gate is being rebuilt where it once stood to show us exactly how the Romans lived when they were here. From the top they could look out over the sea. And the river too, of course.'

The little museum of the Roman Fort was tranquil and carpeted. This room, thought the boy, with awe, is filled with broken stones. With pictures on them. And shattered water pots. When we lived in the village if our mother broke a pot she would weep. When Farida broke the big pot at the well Grandfather saved her from a whipping by telling a lie.

'When it's finished,' said Miss Bagley, tip-tapping the picture against her breast, here and here, 'There will be two tall towers and a fighting platform above the two gates. Just as it was in Roman times. Won't that be a wonderful sight, children? To see it as the Romans saw it?'

Dimly through the walls Class Four could sense the rumble of the cement mixer and the voices of the masons echoed in the doorway. From the river a ship's siren sounded. Miss Bagley looked expectantly at the children about her feet. When she moved the boy saw there was a crescent moon carved into the stone behind her.

Car-lid', Miss Bagley was saying sharply: missing her tea and biscuit in the sanctuary of the staffroom: 'Car-lid, have you heard a single word I've said? Shall I sit you with the girls?'

With eyes and lashes like that, thought Miss Bagley, softening, who would know, and smiled, hushing the girls' giggles with a warning finger.

She cannot even say my name, thought the boy, sadly. I am not Car-lid. I will not answer her. I will sit like the stones and keep silence.

'Car-lid, I'm asking you a question? Do you understand me, Car-lid?'

'He's a Paki, miss. They're too stupid to know English.'

'Who is Paki?' cried the boy, 'Omani! Omani! My father is an important man on tankership!' which was true or untrue depending on how one valued an engineroom artificer.

'You told us your Da was drownded dead.'

Which was the plain truth. If you discounted the smart bomb.

'You live with your Granda, you said.'

'That's enough,' said the teacher, angrily, 'More than enough! You ought to be ashamed of yourself, Wayne,' and to the boy, gently, 'Have you been paying attention, Car-lid?'

'Moon on the stone,' said the boy, pointing.

'Why, yes,' said Miss Bagley, snatching at his discovery as a drowning engineroom artificer grasps a burning liferaft, 'So there is!'

Turning to the children, she said, 'Car-lid's people were here too in Roman days. The boatmen who managed the river for the Romans were from the Persian Gulf. From the great rivers, the Tigris and Euphrates. They came here to live and work, raise families. They died and were buried here. In the graveyard of the vicus, that's the settlement. They were the first in an honoured tradition of seamen, pilots, and foyboatmen. D'you remember the funeral stone I showed you of Regina? Her husband Barates commissioned that stone. He was an Arab. And so men like Car-lid's father, like many of your fathers, have been sailing in and out of the River Tyne ever since.'

Miss Bagley made a mental note to arrange a pastoral visit to Car-lid's family. How long had the boy been in school? Weeks? Months. She felt suddenly guilty that she hadn't made the effort earlier. Perhaps a phone call to Welfare to check whether the boy's father was a war casualty? But now because she was a conscientious and caring teacher she seized the opportunity to explain to Class Four how evil and malicious was the racism of their elders while Simpson lounged in the corner of the museum and disagreed with every single word.

I have found the place, thought the boy, now I have the answer.

Kitty Fitzgerald

Kitty Fitzgerald is the author of four novels:
Pigtopia (Faber, 2005), *Small Acts of Treachery*
(Brandon, 2002), *Snapdragons* (Brandon,
1999) and *Marge* (Sheba, 1985); a poetry
collection: *For Crying Out Loud* (IRON Press,
1994) with Valerie Laws; and four plays for
the BBC and eight theatre plays. She was a
finalist (second place) in the Barnes & Noble
Discover Great New Writers Award in 2005;
received a Hawthornden Fellowship in 2005, a
Time to Write Award in 2003, and a C.P. Taylor
Playwriting Bursary; and won most original
screenplay for the film *Dream On* at Le Baule
Film Festival. Born in Ireland, she lives
on Tyneside.

The Herb Gardener Talks of Basil

She calls it the corpse plant
with its cloven flowers
and cloying sweetness.
I sprinkle it on floors
to discourage flies
and still the mind.
She says it only grows
on the wings of a curse,
whispered as it's sown
in fresh turned earth.
I cure stomach aches
and monthly cramps
with its infusion.
She says it will not flourish
in this northern land,
where frost is intolerant
to its need of warmth.
I have built glass shelters here
where the sun can rest for

more than half a day, new shoots
are pushing through.
She's suspicious of my herb seeds,
brought on galleys up the estuary,
from Rome, to this outcrop.
I offer her bay leaves for luck;
imagine her unclothed
between lavender-scented sheets,
her coarse skin soothed
with oil of olives,
resin of sweet juniper
burning on a charcoal coil.

She drops the plant at my feet,
strides away before
our hands can meet,
towards her ragged hills
which rise like waves
towards the sky.

On Ravenglass

The soil is layered deep with dusty remnants
of the Bathhouse. Viridian glass, fragments of
red jasper, horn, enamel, are pressed between
the delicate bones of small, long-dead creatures.

In Spring, the scent of Thyme seeps through
veined earth, lingers on the salted wind, blows
across a sea which carries still, threats and
promises from the Celtic heartland.

Knowing

We know the wind on the sea
and what it tells
we know soil, silt, sand,
the singing spells
of shape-shifters.

When the hen crowed like a cock
and dog lay down with cat
we knew these omens of ill-luck.

Next sunrise, the Eagle flag
rose over the hill,
horses and foot soldiers
set up camp, plundered
ash and elder for their fires.

We mixed pigments,
painted our skin battle-blue,
twined beads and feathers
into our hair, chanted
till the full fall of night:

thought is swifter than wind
truth is clearer than water

Building a Roman Wall
in the North Lands

Select your route with adequate care,
be aware of Celt and Pictish trails,
their fondness for attacks through bracken,
plan it straight as the eagle flies,
remove plants, trees, grass,
do not dwell on thoughts of home
or your wife's swelling belly.
Dig trenches deep enough
to hide a sleeping hound
and wide enough to march
men close, yet ten abreast,
forget the years you will not witness
pass across your daughter's face.
Line the dug out ground with
smallish stones, up to the height
of your baby's knee, cover to the rim
with grit and gravel, pressed and stamped
to firmness, to withstand the bitter frosts,
the cold which penetrates your veins.
Curve the surface of the road
sufficiently, so rain can drain into
the ditches on each side, move on,
until you reach the fringe of Pictland,
slake your thirst with red grape wine
infused with Rosemary and Thyme.
Build a wall.

Extracts from a Herbalist's Notebook

For tired labourers an infusion
to lift the spirits:

place one ounce of Borage in a
pre-warmed earthstone bowl,
with one half ounce of Rue,
its leaves still bluish-green.
Stir in good measures of
warm water, upwards of one pint,
leave overnight, covered with muslin,
until the cloth is stained emerald
and tangy with the scent of cucumber.
Strain at dawn, through fresh honeycomb,
with the moon still in the sky.
Sip throughout the day, till the sun dips
and acrobating swallows twirl
above the creeping tide.

For soldiers returning injured after battle:
a concoction to discourage bruising:

pulp the fresh seeds of Caraway
until powdery as new fallen snow,
mix with water heated by the sun,
make into a paste, spread thickly
on the wounds while warm,
cover with strips of woven cloth,
soaked well in Marigold,
till the sharpness stings the skin
and the blood is cooled.

For galley crews in need of rest:

place bunches of just-picked Bay into a steaming bath,
crushing the pungent glands along its leaves
with nutmegs to release the oily scent.
Add saffron stigmas, up to three,
have them soak and breathe
the vapours for one hour.
After, burn dried Lavender to aid
a night and day long sleep.

For children suffering pinching stomach pains:

at sunrise, infuse one full hand of the flowers and
leaves of Coriander, with two sprigs of sweetest Basil,
add in three clusters of Valerian from loamy soil.
Steep through the passage
of one whole day, whispering
the child's name every hour.
Strain the following dusk, through fine linen,
add one leaf of Mint and four peppercorns,
dose liberally until the ache subsides.

Defence ditch →
Photo: Steve Chettle

Robert Forsythe

Robert Forsythe is a freelance writer based
in Northumberland. His background is in
both Industrial Archaeology and Theology,
and these inform his investigations into the
industrial and moral aspects of Hadrian's Wall,
and into the links between them. He has a
particular interest in W. H. Auden, especially
his deep involvement with the Northern
Pennines, and with Alan Myers is the joint
author of *W. H. Auden: Pennine Poet.*

An Industrial Archaeologian
upon Hadrian's Wall

Archaeology like society
is rather stratified.
Traditionally the older the archaeology
the more glorious the archaeologist.

Industrial archaeology was
too modern to be real
and its demands
too daunting to realize.

Fashions change.
More visitors went to Beamish.
The Romans became boring.
Marine archaeology in snorkel and wet suit hit TV.

Archaeological taste,
like the society it serves,
tends to specialize (read divisiveness)
which is why catholic tastes are my dish.

The Romans built roads, walls,
bridges, even cornmills,
here on their frontier.
They quarried, worked stone.

Skills that Northumbrian bastle makers,
Georgian house builders, leadminers,
farm dykers, railway navvies were all to share
here in the coming centuries.

I have never been an actor,
dressing up as a legionary
re-enacting conflict makes me nervous
but I am fascinated by tolerance

and how a world class object
visible from space
might be a fulcrum
between inclusivity and exclusion.

Should it celebrate division
between barbarism and civilization?
A gay man concluded
'Whoever deprives an unoffending man of his right is a barbarian'.

He was writing of Hadrian's Wall
and how what separated the barbarian and the Roman
was that the latter did not leave
the scene of the crime but made it home.

That is the essence of the imperial spirit.
Now we live in a post-age.
Post-empire, post-modern, post-nationalisation,
even post-GPO.

Will our email and internet,
our chat rooms and moderators
teach us tolerance
just as Hadrian's Wall
strides across the neck of Britain?

A neck that is largely a quiet landscape
telling of past vulcanology.
But as is proper to a microcosm
the counterpoint to Burgh Marsh
was (is, will be?) at Wallsend.

Saxon style at Corbridge or Ovingham,
Armstrong violence at Housesteads,
George Stephenson's railway,
Alex Glasgow's songs,
Which do you want to celebrate?

They are all together
in the lee of the Wall.
I know what I want:
Peace in Our Time
and a station on the border at Gilsland.

Photo: Melanie Ashby

Linda France

Linda France was born in Wallsend. After some time living away, she moved back to the North East in 1981. She currently lives half a mile south of the Wall, near Stagshaw, Northumberland. Her poetry collections are published by Bloodaxe Books and include *The Simultaneous Dress* (2002) and *The Toast of the Kit Cat Club* (2005), a biography in verse of the eighteenth-century traveller and letter writer Lady Mary Wortley Montagu. Linda also edited *Sixty Women Poets* (Bloodaxe 1993). She teaches Creative Writing at the University of Newcastle upon Tyne.

Found at Portgate

A willing prisoner I spend all day
digging stones out of the earth
like potatoes black with loam and cold
Some too big for me to lift alone

Dressed rectangles or chiselled curves
I wonder if what I'm digging up is Rome
Refugees from Dere Street across the fields
or the Wall hiding behind the Military Road

I handle them with barbarian irreverence
deaf to the drumroll of leather on paving
the comings and goings of Empire
More concerned with the triumvirate

of snow buntings in the leafless rowan
and whether we'll have enough flat stones
to edge the new pond still just
a dark brown apostrophe against the grass

The Love Potion of Polemios

Engraved on a ring found at Corbridge, now in the British Museum

*

He wouldn't tell me what was in it.
It tasted of river, a tang of trout
with a trickle of heat under it,
wine to help it slip down gently.
It slipped down gently as a willow
                    coming into leaf.

*

I dreamt of gloves and shoes, the finest hide,
a second skin. Waking up was like dancing.
The sun lifted the sleep out of my hair
and I was up with the squirrels. Naked
as a baby. Hungry as a slave. Eyes
                    dry as kindling.

*

The first time I saw him I was a bird,
all feathers and song. From up there
on the balcony I saw the sun
turn his hair to bronze as he walked.
I lost all power of flight. My face burned.
Couldn't tell if the heat was his or mine.
He didn't look up. I swear if he did
                    I would have gone blind.

*

Crowned and tawny, my lion heart.
Something gold about his eyes. He looks at me
slowly and I glisten. Makes me wait
till the sun is an arrow in the sky.
The best omen. He is the Emperor
of Amber, and I am a fly
                    locked in yellow light.

*

He invented magnetism. Science
was on his side. He brings me a bowl
of April, its lip so curved and gentle,
I catch fire. It takes an hour to get used
to the dazzle. We both powder into ash,
                    thinking of nothing but water.

*

The claw of morning. His early hungry rays.
Water and wine. A craving for trout.

Photo: Steve Chettle

Penny Grennan

Penny Grennan is an experienced writer and writing tutor. She was brought up in East and Central Africa and has a background in Education and English Literature and Language. She has worked extensively in community settings, teaching journalism and creative writing, as well as setting up writing festivals and poetry readings.

She enjoys wordplay and irony and champions the pun in both her personal and professional life. She also likes the 'snapshot' potential of poetry. In addition to travelling and collecting, she has an interest in archaeology and public transport, both of great importance to the Romans – past and present.

Triolet

The Romans march across our land
The hillsides echo with their feet
They offer a protective hand
The Romans march across our land
Their conquest has been carefully planned
The Romans march across our land
The hillsides echo with their feet

Authority gives them the right
To conquer, murder or befriend
They come in legions through the night
Authority gives them the right
To conquer hearts without a fight
On our agreement they depend
Authority gives them the right
To conquer, murder or befriend

The wall is where I live my life
With northern wind that blows with rage
It cuts at England like a knife
The wall is where I live my life
Exposed to elemental strife
Which time does little to assuage
The wall is where I live my life
With northern wind that blows with rage

We live in an uneasy peace
The days have multiplied to years
They pay no rent, they have no lease
We live in an uneasy peace
Will occupation ever cease
And free us from our constant fears?
We live in an uneasy peace
The days have multiplied to years.

Cleanliness is Next to Godliness

Which God?
How clean?
Which unguents
Will guarantee
That I'm next
In the line
To shake His hand?
I hope he has washed
before I hold it.

In the Bathhouse 10.20 pm

It is late and I shouldn't be here
But the dirt of days has ingrained my skin
Full of stories. I will wash them away
To settle in the silt of centuries.
Each layer will shed light
On the substrate of the past.
Thumb print flecks, depositing a record
Of all the washing that has gone before.

Tired men, bone ached with work,
Sigh in the balm of warm water
Their parchment hides telling tales of tanning
The tide of calm softening their mood before sleep.

The bathhouse is silent with fatigue
And I am dreaming of the sky.

Line of Hadrian's Wall

I live on a line
A thin division between now and always.
A boundary, thick with blood.
It is a high line
Drawn with the ink of glory.
A precipice for men to step over,
Punished for going too far.
The wind of years
Batters the line
But it never wavers.
It is all that has happened and all that remains.
I live on a line.
I am careful to toe it.

Stone for St Oswald Hill Head Farm

Went out again late last night
Sneaking through the corners of the dark
To collect more stone.
Why? I don't know,
But I feel like a thief
Plundering the past.

My neighbour takes what he needs
In broad daylight.
Brass neck.
But me? No!
I creep across the boundary of right and wrong
To steal stones that belong to the dead.

It is only by taking what isn't mine
That I wonder
Who do these stones belong to anyway?

However, I shall still do my stealing in the dark.

An Interest in Public Transport

How do you measure
The movement of troops
From A to B
When the telephone has not been invented
And Morse code
Is still a pulse in someone's heart?
How do you know your rations are sufficient
To fill the mouths of invading armies
Hungry for glory?
How do you know they have gathered enough
To keep them alive
Through unknown territory?

You need to measure the footfall
Of an average man
Multiplying it by the hours of walking
Walking straight and narrow
Carving supply lines across the empire.
You try to avoid the delay of Sir Galahad
When the temperature is soaring.
You keep to a schedule
And hope that the post arrives on time.

A Report from the Border

Nothing to report except the same
We walk, we stop, we work, we play,
Nothing to report except the same
We build and dig until the end of day,
Nothing to report except the same
Small differences over food or pay,
Nothing to report except the same
Gods multiplying and all we do is pray
And freeze and fight and do not disobey
So that there is always
Nothing to report except the same.

View from Housesteads →
Photo: Kate Still/ARTS UK

Photo: Stephanie E R Mickler

Bill Herbert

Bill Herbert was born in Dundee in 1961,
and was educated there and at Oxford,
where he completed his DPhil thesis on
Hugh MacDiarmid (published as *To Circumjack
MacDiarmid* by OUP in 1992). He has published
seven collections of poetry, the last five with
Bloodaxe, and his books have received many
accolades, including three Scottish Arts
Council awards, and have been shortlisted
for most of the major British poetry prizes.
In 2000 he edited *Strong Words: modern
poets on modern poetry*, with Matthew Hollis.
His most recent collection, *Bad Shaman Blues*,
is a Poetry Book Society recommendation.
He teaches Creative Writing and Contemporary
Poetry at Newcastle University, and lives in
a former lighthouse in North Shields.

dis manibus

when all scrolls fail
and what survives of script
is chiselled on graves

when stone is stolen
and bones lose names
we're only, wholly here

our spirits deify
this landscape by
departing into it

our spirits defy
the glutting flow
and hide in glimpses

momentary fanes,
this cult of peripherals, where
gliff must stand for glyph

an alphabet of tracks:
claws and soles
hooves and paws

parochial recoveries:
the dialect of touch
the elegies of water

Song of the Shieldsmen

From Merzbau to Mithraeum
we march along this wall:
if we saw Picts we'd slay them
but Picts are bloody small.

They've got into our bloodstream
they've got inside our heads,
we think we're pigging Latin
we're pigging Picts instead.

There's Pictish on our bus tickets
there's Pict yeast in our bread,
and when we march upon this wall
there's Picts climb in our beds.

Our sperms have nanoPicts attached
that leap onto our eggs,
and when we march through marshy grass
we've leech-Picts on our legs.

A Pict is everything we hate
because we've never known:
from Dada art to the feel of Fate,
a Pict's what we can't own.

A Pict's the thing that lives upon
the tongue-tip of our doubt,
a Pict's the virus of our dreams
we drown out with this shout:

From Mithraeum to Merzbau
we fear they will attack,
so when we've marched from there to here
we turn and march right back.

Over the Wall

1

When you drive the road that cuts to Carlisle
year-long, from week to week in parallel
to that constrictor's vertebrae, the Wall;
from its disjointed jaws that try to swallow
all the Tyne like a gazelle, past
old Cuddy's Crags, the Whin Sill;
glancing north to where in autumn and in evening
the light begins to strip the local greens away
in favour of a brittle ochre hue,
you start to feel the Romans got the border right.

2

True Wall, magnetic Wall,
Wall that never mentions North
but hints obliquely like an only line:
here begins beyond.

Here all thought of borders was born
to the west of empire,
swaddled in vallum and cribbed with stone,
where before they had let their sense of limits
seep through the babble:
horribilesque ultimosque Britannos

Here men began to hold the shrinking world
that had held them
upon her unbound breasts.

3

You start to think it's like a mirror
that you somehow escaped through with
a book held in your trailing hand
that sticks in the liminal air as though across bars.

You want to plead, 'O wall,
O sweet and lovely wall,
through whom I see my bliss, let all
my drag of luggage pass', until,
spine first, high as hawks, the book begins to appear,
steadying there at the end of your kitestring arm.

The difficult words can't make it through,
their letters swoop and clatter in the grass like armour;
their questions fall on the other side
of the unguarded Wall, their great marks sprawl
untranslated in the barbaric grass:
armis/reddidit aeratis sonitum

Antinous of the Tyne

Ignore the statues. Here we have you,
floating face down, not searching Tyne
    for divinity,
      not looking at all,
just floating that marble-firm backside,
  those white thighs splayed in brown.

You died in Egypt, in that huge gap
between the facts called intimacy
    or perhaps the Nile,
      so what's washed you here
beneath our noses at Arbeia
  must be a myth like love.

Some crocodile's flung your guts around
before you got here, or the fingers
    of Hadrian have
      sought out soft omens
caresses couldn't yield, that you'd pass
  passion's liquid thresholds.

Your curls are drenched in more than perfume
and your lips pout with a darker stain,
    a greater vintage
      makes your cheeks hectic
than the supply ship brings: you've joined those
  the gods are sorry died.

Osiris, Dionysus, Hermes:
your soul was told to dwell with them, by
    your emperor, in
      a glut of temples,
a cult flowing like a river past
  the waiting banks of faith.

Those unreflective shores, anxious to
observe their latest rites whether you
    wept into silks with
      joy or not, ageing
with the hard breath of your master on
  your nape, not twenty yet.

Ignore the statues that piece your moods
together, like a mosaic they tramped
    upon for decades:
      concentrate on coins
that hold your godhead, still in the mouths
  of Danube, Tyne, like teats.

Esther Jansma

Esther Jansma, who is an archaeologist as
well as a poet, made her debut in 1988 with
Stem onder mijn bed (*Voice under my Bed*),
followed by *Bloem, steen* (*Flower, Stone*, 1990)
and her much-acclaimed third collection,
Waaigat (1993). Her fourth book, *Picknick op
de wenteltrap* (*Picnic on the Spiral Staircase*,
1997), is written from the perspective of a
small child. *Hier is de tijd* (*Time Is Here*, 1998)
was awarded the prestigious VSB Poetry Prize
in 1999, and *Dakruiters* (*Spires*, 2000) won
the Hugues C. Pernath Prize in 2001. Her most
recent collection is *Alles is nieuw* (*Everything
is New*, 2005). In 2006 she received the
A. Roland Holst Award for her complete
oeuvre. A selection of her work in English
translation by Francis R. Jones will appear
from Bloodaxe in 2007.

Translations on pages 50, 51 and 52 by Francis R Jones

The House

Even after the Romans people pass.
Someone (imagined) in Carlisle, 2004:

The sounds belong to my ears, the doors
belong to my hands, the red tiles
to my eyes, the floors to my daughters and
the attics to my sons and vice versa

it all belongs to me, I live as I sleep
beneath the safe roof of my breathing
until the wind shakes up the walls,
forgets the tiles with my sight and falls still.

It will be another wind blowing through the house.
Maybe you are still here, and maybe not.
It will be another wind blowing through the house.

Someone has a house, the sounds belong
to her ears, the doors belong to her hands,
but it is not me. We are not there.

The Beginning

Roman glass, Housesteads

Suddenly she saw the size of the world.
Nothing was the way she had expected
things were fuller than she had thought

and more colourful, by looking through
the glass that had found her she saw
the inside of shells; what moved through it

was form and utterly itself and all
the while a rainbow of possibilities
blown into life and lost and found again

after the ages had painted their mother-
of-pearl across it, ever so fragile
and there it lay, just like that in her hand.

128 AD

I come from the mud, with cohorts
up to my eyes in sublunary shite
I've razed forests, repaved and rerouted roads,
rebuilt the Imperial Border. The places I've seen,

pal, soft as porridge the soil there: you drown
in sludge, you dine on swill, your billet's a one-
arsed village of mud slapped into bricks and dried...
Not that the bloody sun ever shines there –

it's turned its miserable face away
hides in a slate-grey crying fit of mist
more rain, vicious, pissing, remorseless
than you could ever believe – but

the crack was good as well. Plenty of blondes,
Batavian whores. Who bleat or is it moo
as you're screwing them. As for their grasping
hard-and-fast fingers, fair enough - I had the cash.

And then the crossing, worked on the wall
hand of a god who keeps us safe and warm.
The job is done. I stayed on: I live in clover
here in the glow of this stone hand's palm

that reddens as I write. Sunset
casts on these grasslands what look like
old hills, the clouds above are new,
the shades of night close in. I wait.

Wall

On the 'right' side of whatever wall

It is the way we say it is, simply
here and us, here in our wide-open house
built of landscape, grass we understand
and graze, water, roads, fields of grain.

Crystal-clear places filled with stars and gods
are our roof and here all actions speak for
themselves – and so they must, there's no room
here for what has remained untamed, unknown.

And yet beyond the meandering border of this
thinking, the mortared project labelled we, the enemy's
always waiting and I don't know him, he won't fit

inside this head, this order, the nowadays in which
I live as if in a night that's filled with danger and din
and close the windows which keep on blowing open.

The Collector

Excavations under way at Hadrian's Wall

This was not found in some attic but down
at rock bottom like things left behind after
a modern death, limp neglected tat
in the hands of the heir, myself, collector.

What drives me into the depths is not a desire for
something higher, it's little and insolent, picking up
clothes the dustman left behind – turned to uneven
paving, rain-stained – to know what it was like.

It's scrabbling, chasing the vanishing,
people of the past, shards of thought,
sequences which led to action - planing wood,

cutting out little clothes – moments long ago,
which really were and which are really
vanished till someone grasps them, reads them back.

Esther Jansma at Housesteads →
Photo: Steve Chettle

Kapka Kassabova

Kapka Kassabova is a poet, novelist, travel writer, and professionally displaced person. Born and bred in Bulgaria, she was educated at a French lycée in Sofia and two New Zealand universities. Since 1992 she has been based mainly in New Zealand, but two years ago she moved to Britain and lives in Edinburgh.

Her first poetry book, *All Roads Lead to the Sea*, won a NZ Montana Book Award. Her novel *Reconnaissance* (Penguin NZ), won the 2000 Commonwealth Writers' Prize for best first novel in the Asia-Pacific category. She was the 2002 and 2004 NZ Cathay Pacific Travel Writer of the Year. In 2002–03, she held the Creative NZ Berlin Writer's Residency. She is the author of two Globetrotter Guides and also writes for BBC radio. Her latest book is *Someone Else's Life* (Bloodaxe).

Roman Whore Blues

This is the end of the world. The rain is like a flood.
My lover's in that city thirsty for wine and blood.

They brought me across to sodden Britannia
And here we met – he from Thrace, I from Mauritania.

In my leather strips, with callused feet,
I am the centurions' favourite meat.

Life here is brutish, cold and sad.
So he went to be famous in Rome, or dead.

Again, they'll throw him to tigers and men.
And if he dies, I'll never laugh again.

And then I'll die too, and be buried with no stone.
Words and stones are for the rich alone.

On this bowl is our story, I'll bury it later:
VERECUNDA ACTRESS LUCIUS GLADIATOR

The inscription in this poem was found on a pottery fragment in Leicester. Otherwise these poems were written around inscriptions, tablets and tombstones along the Wall. The Roman text appears in capitals.

Letter from Claudia Severa to Sulpicia Lepidina

Briga, 100 AD

CLAUDIA SEVERA TO HER LEPIDINA GREETINGS
JUST AS I HAD SPOKEN WITH YOU
AND PROMISED THAT I WOULD ASK BROCCHUS
AND THAT I WOULD COME TO YOU
I DID ASK HIM AND HE REPLIED
THAT IT IS ALWAYS WHOLEHEARTEDLY
PERMITTED TO ME TO COME TO YOU WHATEVER WAY I CAN
THERE ARE CERTAIN INTIMATE MATTERS WHICH...
I long to discuss with you. I suspect
my Brocchus wants to send me off so he can take up
with the Barbarian redhead who hangs around the fort
her hair shamelessly loose.
She set her sights on Brocchus last September.
And I'm a fool for loving him so much.
And is your Cerialis faithful? How is your little son?
I lost a child last month, it just bled out.
Life is either boring or painful, sister.

And if we're lucky, the future will make
verse of our letters, shopping lists and deaths.
Vindolanda will fall, another Caesar will rule,
our unborn children will die. And yet we have to try.
Meanwhile, ON THE 11 OF SEPTEMBER, SISTER
FOR THE CELEBRATION OF MY BIRTHDAY
I GIVE YOU A WARM INVITATION
YOU WILL MAKE THE DAY MORE ENJOYABLE
BY YOUR PRESENCE
GREET YOUR CERIALIS
FAREWELL MY SISTER
MY DEAREST AND MOST LONGED-FOR SOUL

Claudia Severa and Sulpicia Lepidina, both officers' wives,
had a correspondence around 100 AD while Lepidina lived at Vindolanda
for four years. There are two known tablets which record their correspondence,
both from Claudia Severa, and here I have combined them into one.

Farewell I Wish That
You Are Very Happy

I'm sitting on a river bench. The plaque reads:
he lived, laughed, loved, and left.

And after him, things still grew from the Wall –
trees, houses, weather, childish summers,

winter mornings quick with hope and frost
as if for the first time,

cobwebs of electricity hummed overhead, the river
and the sky moved in the same direction,

past Vindolanda where a man called Maior wrote
I'M WARMING THE BED AS I WRITE TO YOU

past this bench where I receive the letter
though it's not addressed to me

no, such destinations are not for us, only their ruins –
the lone children of our love and laughter. And that's it.

Barely I have the time to make a note of this.
Barely he had the time to write

FAREWELL I WISH THAT YOU ARE VERY HAPPY

The Past and Future of
Aurelius Marcus

Carvoran means nothing now.
The milecastle is gone.
But the lichen remains on the stones
to prove that here stood a man
called Aurelius Marcus
turned to the north where nothing grew
but wind and hairy Picts. He took a piss.

The plague was in the south, far away.
His wife in bed, his children too.
His soldiers shivered under the moon
played dice, and were lucky
not to know the future. The past
is another story.

Somewhere in between, Aurelius Marcus
pays a stone carver and spells
through tears and rain the chiselled words:
SHE WAS MY VERY PURE WIFE
WHO LIVED THIRTY THREE YEARS
WITHOUT BLEMISH

Angela Locke

Angela Locke is a poet, novelist and journalist
living in Cumbria, whose books have been
translated all over the world. She broadcasts
widely on television and radio, and writes two
feature columns for the magazine *Cumbria
Life*. Angela has a Creative Writing MA in
Poetry/Prose and The Writer as Tutor from
Northumbria University. She divides her time
between writing, teaching Creative Writing
and running international Writing Retreats.
A new edition of her first book, *Mr Mullett
Owns a Cloud* (Chatto & Windus), is to be
published in 2006 by Cumbria Life Books.

Fibula

Senhouse Museum, Maryport

Some craftsman beat this tine into a curve,
Wrought this clasp with curlicues, butter in a farmer's basket.
It must have been a loved thing in this barren place, far from home.
A gift to a woman. There is some love here, in this simple thing,
An ordered, crafted chaos in this copper pin, too light for winter cloaks.
Some lady of the town cared for it, used it to pin her lighter gowns
On rare days in the North when it was warm enough for summer finery.
Roman holidays when the legions drilled, new altars consecrated,
Slaves bought, an air of festival around the vicus,
The scent of aromatic fires, saffron and juniper,
Lavender from the old country, fresh pies baked at dawn.
She wore that new brooch he had given her to complement
The cloth brought from Rome on muleback. And a woman
In the Roman crowd, hand on soft-downed arm,
Had said 'My dear, so delicate.'

Now the tiny thing is lost; a trifle.
Light cloth snagging on a doorway, the pin
Was wrenched away, lies still in earth,
Under some stone, forever separate.
The brooch fell without your noticing.
You grieved a little.
For centuries, it lay here in the ground,
The sea wind turning art to dust.
It's cold now in my hand, exuding dampness,
Copper marking my palm. Stigmata
Of forgotten lives.

Miss O'Connor's Wall

Beyond the playground wall
Miss O'Connor walks among the roses
We spy on her through the half-dead tree
In the corner of the path

Furtive   admiring
We watch our headmistress
Off-duty   as she glides elegantly
Among the blooms
A trug held in the crook of her arm
Black hair clipped in a perfect bun

The charm of it
Is the secret assignation we have with her
Half admiring   half in awe

Conscious of our imperfections
Our dusty plimsolls jammed into wall cracks
Fingers digging into soil   we watch   sweating
Dirt under our fingernails

Girls who will never be perfect
Who will always be a disappointment
Have played rough in the playground
Bullied the fat girl in the Nissen hut
Carried out arcane ceremonies
Sworn the worst swearing

Dared

We are forever outsiders
Beyond Miss O'Connor's wall
As she bends her elegant head
To smell the perfect rose

Our books a smudge of ink and finger marks
We are marked as failures in her Book of Life.

I Walk Among the Grief of Trees

I have seen enough death in my service
To the Emperor. It never moved me,
Made me a good soldier.
I could stand in carnage, give clear orders,
Was commended by our commanders.

Yet where I stand now on this Wall's ending,
Close to the turning of the sea,
The scent of living air comes to me from far
Beyond the boundary, the place of the barbarian.
A north wind, the stirring of change, death.

I remember my mother opening the house doors
As the north wind swept through the village.

I never should have visited the whores.
They bring disease, even the officers' whores
Are unclean. They say the woman
Had been a chieftain's wife, a priestess
In the old ways, from beyond the Wall.

A bow's length into the forest,
Where the necessary destruction had taken place,
She had laid down in front of the foot soldiers,
A futile protest at the cutting of the trees.

Of course they took her.

We tolerate the pagan ways. They are wild,
Unkempt, these people beyond the Wall.
They do not have the baths, nor laws as we do,
Worship gods of superstition.

But it's the same everywhere.
Thank Jupiter for Rome bringing a little civilization.
It is a great comfort to be a citizen
Of a civilized country.

It was rumoured in the bathhouse
That the woman has cast spells.
It makes everything more dangerous.
Now she is my house slave. While I am kind,
She, the barbarian, holds me cruelly,
She makes me rut her like a stag a hind,
And will not look upon my Roman face.

The breath of the green wind taunts me.
I remember my mother opening all the doors
Of the house, sweeping Death from the place.

The slave woman is sending me dreams.
As I suck her paps, she becomes the Wolf
Who fed Rome. I am haunted by portents.
I see the corpses of ancient trees, some future
War, a land churned to mud. I walk
Among the grief of trees.
There will be no greening in the Spring.
A perpetual winter light streams down
On us.

My eyes are open.

The wind comes to me
From the North, and the sea to the West turns.
Tomorrow I will make a sacrifice to Jupiter.
It will ease my mind.

After the Raj; Last Outpost of the Empire

It's February at the Wall's end,
The turning of the sea.
No longer under military control,
Gulls lift in a free wind.

The Romans have gone.
They've left their roads behind.
Their Wall. We're grateful.

This Raj once had fine buildings,
Mimicking temples, statues of worthies
Staring out at horizons,
A sense of awe in local populations.

Empires must be good eventually.
They leave their laws behind,
Are generally benign in their effect,
Use power wisely.

The old lie.

What is left here along the Wall
Is so much a whisper of itself
It's hard to catch; slavery, abuse,
Those racial taunts against the Britons,
Second-class citizens of subjugated lands,
Cannon fodder in Empire's unrelated wars.
The way to power still apes
The Raj, taking over bungalows,
Government offices, adopting the religion
Of rulers, speaking their language
Better than they did themselves.

Of course the Romans were so long ago,
Hardly a stone stands.
Few tracks of them remain,
No empire of the powerful,
No dispossessed,
Who do not know the language
Of the victors.

Yet, Empire to Empire, some things
More enduring than the track
Of ancient Walls
Have stayed the same.

Ellen Phethean

Ellen Phethean is a sound artist, poet, playwright and editor, who co-founded Diamond Twig press with Julia Darling. Her poetry is in *Sauce* (Bloodaxe Books) and has been broadcast on BBC Radios 3 and 4. She has written plays for radio, Northumbria University, Live Theatre's Youth Group and schools. In 2003–04 she was writer-in-residence at Seven Stories in Newcastle and wrote *Wall*, a teen novel in poems, to be published by Smokestack Books. She is currently working on another novel in similar style. She teaches Writing for Children at the Centre for Lifelong Learning in Newcastle.

Wall

Five extracts from her long poem

Kylie

I often stare out
me bedroom window: I can see
a gang of lads and lasses: they look small
from up here. They hang about, nothing to do
nowhere to go, cannot kick a ball even
so they sit, wait, smoke, swear, laugh and drink
scaring the bairns, the old folks as they call out.
Mam says they're animals, they're not, nah.
She says it's a jungle, the bushes grow too tall
you might get jumped on by chavas
rapists, smackheads, or what all.
People say it's rough. Nah, it's not that bad
I should kna, I live here, in the Byker Wall.

Sean's Tag

Attention Deficit Hyperactivity Disorder, Dyslexia, Special Needs
Removal Unit, Caution, Custody, Persistent Youth Offender, Acceptable
Behaviour Agreement, Criminal Damage, Racially Aggravated Burglary,
Anti Social Behaviour Order, Crime and Disorder Act, Anger
Management Course, Intensive Supervision

Sean's head swims with words
they've always been his enemy
won't stay still on the page
like black demons or matchstick men
that hop in front of his eyes, like fleas
teasing him, moving their little letters about
making a fool of him, making others laugh at him
infuriating him.
Until he discovered a way to make them do what he wanted.

If the page was big enough, the letters bold enough
the colours not black, but crimson, emerald, silver and jet
with spray paint and a blank wall
Sean could write his tag, his name
with care, detail, artistic flair.
A'CEE
and other words too, words the whole of Newcastle could read.

School, the Polis, Adults, Everyone
said he was no good, a failure, the worst.
So Sean said Right, I'll be the Best
at being Bad.
It is his message to the world.

Nana Invites Mrs Jayasinha Round

There's a soft knocking on Nana's door,
standing there is a small bird
of a woman, cinnamon skin
slight as a feather
wreathed in amber cloth,
wearing a shell necklace.
'Come in, come in', says Nana,
she's an eager highland terrier
welcoming her neighbour. She points
'Mother of Pearl we call that, it's a beautiful wee thing'
'Thank you, thank you'
Mrs Jayasinha puts her palms together
nods her head
'It was given by my mother'
tiny hands hold the shells
up to the window:
'See?'
and shows her fingers, dark stripes
through the delicate silver ovals.

Nana's plump tips
touch it gently, 'I've some china similar'
she reaches into a cupboard, tiptoes
stretches, pulls out her precious
porcelain cup and saucer, with a gold rim,
worn and faded now,
made for dainty tea times long ago.
'This belonged to my grandmother'
Nana hands it to the young woman
enjoys the sight of slim wrists
cradling her family treasure.
Mrs Jayasinha lifts it up
'See?' says Nana.
They look at how it holds light,
empty, weightless
yet full of mystery and promise.
They stare, silent,
not knowing what the other really sees.

Dad Looks Out the Window of His Cree

It's all about desire. Getting the birds to return.
They'll hurry if they know there's a pretty dove
waiting on their perch.

Across the river, I can see the new art gallery
red brick, Baltic in big letters,
I remember when it was a flour mill.
Everything's changed, it's confusing,
the look of things can fool you
like us – married
but it doesn't feel like we are.

There's the millennium bridge, smart folk
walking up and down, looking for something
art I suppose, a new feeling.
We're in different worlds, different universe
like an invisible wall between us:
I don't belong there, and they
never see me.
It feels like that with her, too.
Maybe she can't see a new use
for me?
How is it I can get pigeons to come back
but not my wife?

Life in the Wall

Dad sees
a Vee sign above
geese giving two fingers
to Autumn.

Mam listens to
raised voices in the back lane,
black and yellow bags bulge – lives
thin with stretching too little too far.

Sean loves the whine,
off-road bikes, bad lads
shooting through the estate.

Nana imagines she hears
the rush of waves
in the cars, endlessly passing.

In a high wind
the flat shakes
Kylie
dreams of escape.

The Jayasinha son learns
not to go out
when he hears
lads shout:
TOON TOON
BLACK AND WHITE ARMEE!

Photo: Steve Chettle

Jacob Polley

Jacob Polley was born in Carlisle in 1975 and grew up in Bowness-on-Solway and Burgh-by-Sands. His first book of poems, *The Brink*, published in 2003, was a Poetry Book Society Choice and was shortlisted for the T.S. Eliot Prize. He is the Visiting Fellow Commoner in the Creative Arts at Trinity College, Cambridge, for 2005–07. His second book, *Little Gods*, is due to be published by Picador in December 2006.

Last Year We

bought bags of kindling
and coal at the corner shop,
lit a fire in the black unguarded range,
then daren't leave
when the embers rolled across the kitchen floor;
we cooked leeks in butter,
bathed by candlelight while talking to each other
from the downstairs bathroom
through the open kitchen door;
we had a second fridge for beer,
fairy lights round the mantelpiece for most of the year.
You slept on a mattress,
laundered your shirts
Friday evenings and hung them on the dolly's iron frame,
made toast every day when you came in from work.
I waited, stood at night
watching both ends of the back lane
from our back gate;
passed out in a yellow room
we joked would be good for my disposition:
it wasn't; smoked, drank both bottles of last year's sloe gin
on the sly, wrote nothing.

Dead Leaves and Yellow Light

I catch the first smell of wood smoke
as I walk past the weir.
The water bears the weight
and noise of last night's storm.
The trees are black with rain,
and the cold's risen to hang in the dips
at the bottom of hills, beside the wheat field
and the tyre factory, the railway line
and the bowling green, past Nestlé's plant –
the smell of sour milk –
and my old secondary school,
its broad playing field and cages
where football's played
under the high, white lights in the evenings.

Elder

Don't bring the hollow wood indoors,
but float the flowerheads in tap-water
for two days in a stone crock, then strain
the liquor through muslin, wondering

at the time it takes a ladleful to clarify.
Sugared and stood on a cold larder floor,
one forgotten bottle blows its cork
while you lie with no ideas in the dark.

The Turf-cutter

The turf-cutter folds up his turf
as if you'd caught him breaking camp,
bare earth under his bedroll.

Roman Epitaph

When I died
my husband had me wrapped in a homespun shroud
and paid the mason for a tombstone:

it said I was beautiful and thrifty,
that my skin was like a fresh apricot's.

Soon, those who remembered me differently
also died.

History

Here's what lasts:
the buckles and pins,

the arrowheads,
but not the shafts,

piss-pots, urns, epitaphs,
false teeth; graffiti.

Bust of Hadrian at Chesters Museum →
Photo: Steve Chettle

Photo: Grant Sonnex

Katrina Porteous

Katrina Porteous lives on the Northumberland coast. She has published five collections of poetry, including *The Lost Music* (Bloodaxe Books, 1996), and a book about the Northumbrian fishing community, *The Bonny Fisher Lad* (People's History, 2003). In 2001 her long poem about farming on Hadrian's Wall, 'This Far and No Further', was broadcast on Radio 4. This was followed by 'An Ill Wind', a response to the devastating foot-and-mouth epidemic. Katrina worked again with the farming community for Writing on the Wall, and her poem 'Two Countries' is a snapshot of the aftermath of that epidemic.

Two Countries

This is the oak tree that should not be here.
It stretched its blind shoot from the ungrazed fell last year.
In the spring of no lambs, it fixed its grip on Bradley's,

Snaking pale roots through the soil, a volunteer
To fortune on the bare hill. When it grows tall
And crazed with age, the hiker on the Wall

Above the farm will pass, oblivious
As now to what it means – this doubtful peace,
This border drawn between two warring countries.

The Ruined Thistles

Have loosened their armour.
Their sweat-blackened leather

And tarnished spikes
Shrink, the phalanx

Of glinting weapons,
Disarrayed, softens.

They are losing the fight,
The struggle to stay upright.

Old drunks, their wits
Fly-blown, sour as piss,

They scrabble with dirty nails,
Droop grey heads, spill

Themselves, a filthy
Straggle, and loll

About, their flies undone.
They have turned themselves inside out.

A breeze rustles their hair,
Soothes them. It is the law:

Lambs fatten. Oats
Ripen. Virtue rots

From the inside. Reason
Has finally burst them open.

Their wits fly away like smoke
Into next year, and next.

Hashem Shafiq

Hashem Shafiq was born in Iraq in 1950. He published his first collection of poems in Baghdad in 1973 and worked as a journalist, critic and writer. He left Iraq in 1978 for Paris, later living and working in Beirut, Damascus and Nicosia as a journalist until 1989 when he settled in London, where he lives now with his wife and two children. He has published fourteen collections of poetry to date. He has also edited a selection of Iraqi poetry (Aden, 1984), and published one novel (Beirut, 1992). Many of his poems have been translated into English, French, Kurdish, Persian, German, Italian and Polish, and published in international anthologies. He has recently published his collected poems translated into French, *La Prominade du Cristal*. He also published two volumes of collected poetry in Lebanon in 2005.

Translations on pages 72 and 73 by Hafsa Bekri-Lamrani, and on pages 74 and 75 by Sinan Antoon

A Small Bay

In the middle of a bay
Deserted by waters
Boats and ships stand still
On a muddy bottom.
Blue and white ships
With cracking paint,
Decaying wood and
Parting boards
While foodless seagulls
Cry in the horizon and
The air smells of fish.
Smells that creep under your skin
And carry scents of shore and cords.

Smells of ships that had fed time
Until it turned into water
Until fishermen became
Gods emerging from water,
Branches and beaks
From clay and air.

In the middle of a bay
Invaded by the tide
Water will indeed come back.

Hadrian's Wall

In the first century
There was a Roman King
To whom the stones submitted
And the Rebel land yielded
And the sea
And the blue colour of these skies;

The stars came to accompany him
The moon saluted him and
Descended as a guest to his fort;
The flowers announced his scents;
The trees walked long distances
To salute him;

The eagles landed on his shoulders
The wolves befriended him
And the desert obeyed his tracks.
I see here in Newcastle his
Nickel iron soled sandals, his heavy
Ringmail and his iron cape.
What kind of plundering King is this
who chases out of his capital all the
'Barbarians' of the world and builds
This steady wall in the face of older
Times, against the wind, against
Spears plotting elsewhere?

There was a King
Celebrated by time and
Surrounded by the Horizon.

Waiting

Right here, in the drawer
I put:
apples
bread
and pears.
On the wooden table:
a bottle of Shiraz
a paper cup
glowing with red wine.
In the other drawer
there is white paper
waiting for the words.
Here in Wallsend
close to Roman castles
where history will start
its biography.

A Skeleton at the Arbeia Museum

At the Arbeia museum
amidst tombs of glass
I found the skeleton of an ancient man.
He was smiling
had white teeth
a strong skull
and a ring around his finger
glistening in all directions.
He was lying under the light
free of stress
listening to the music
playing at the museum
amazed
and pure of soul.
He was elegant
celebrating his decaying bones.
I approached to see more.
I saw my own reflection
on the tomb's glass.
I was lying
silent
clean
having been washed by
cares.

The Sun-God Temple

At the temple of Mithras
I listened to silence
purifying my depths
cleansing me of the world's rust,
so much silence
accumulating in this temple.
I prayed with my eyelids
and called through my breaths
so my body parts
would not utter a word.

At the temple of Mithras
I became an entity
that can touch
but is untouchable
I became invisible
intertwined with the first gods
I saw the Romans

digging the unknown
with a golden axe
ploughing the skies with blades
to discover that which is more beautiful
they were the cavalry
occupying horizons
diminishing the distance

At the temple of Mithras
the sun god and its guard
I saw the Romans' torches
wandering in my imagination and my depths
I heard the mooing of the dying bull
killed by Mithras' knife
entering my heart
to rid it of civilian illusions

Photo: Steve Chettle

Samuel Shimon

Samuel Shimon was born into an Assyrian family in Iraq in 1956. He left Iraq in 1979 to go to Hollywood and become a film-maker, and got as far as Damascus, Amman, Beirut, Nicosia, Cairo and Tunis. He settled in Paris in 1985, and has lived in London since 1996. In 2005 his autobiographical novel *An Iraqi in Paris* was published in Arabic and in English translation, and was described by the *Times Literary Supplement* as 'forgiving and powerful' and in *The Independent* as 'always witty and humane'. He is editor of the literary website kikah.com and assistant editor and co-founder of *Banipal* magazine.

Kika and the Ferrymen

An extract from his short story

1

The first time I ever heard the word 'wall'
I was a kid. It was in a very sad song that
my mother used to sing about a train leaving.
One day I asked her why she always sang
such a sad song, and she said that the young
lover was waiting there in the station while
the train carried his loved one far away.
He was sad, like a lonely wall, she said.

2

Sitting in the train from London to Newcastle,
I was thinking about Hadrian's Wall, and
found myself little by little remembering the
poem by W. H. Auden, 'Roman Wall Blues',
which is one of only a very few of his poems
translated into Arabic.

3

Standing at the mouth of the river Tyne, I said to myself: 'You are
merely a tourist, jumping from one place to another in this geography
that is completely new to you.' I was standing on ground that was white
with snow, with the squawking of the seagulls mixing with the
resonance of all the new names I was hearing – Tyne, South Shields,
Wallsend, Chollerford, Corbridge, Chesters, Newburn, Northumberland,
Hadrian's Wall, Arbeia Fort, Brampton, Heddon, Hexham, Haydon Bridge,
Vindolanda Fort...

I was eating fish and chips and hearing a voice telling me: 'Your
ancestors were working here. They were ferrymen from the Tigris.'
I was nodding my head and saying, yes, my ancestors were slaves here.
Slaves under this same sky.

4

When I say 'my ancestors' I can think only of my father. I don't like
to go further back than him. My father is all my ancestors. And for me,
he is always that deaf-dumb skinny man. He was in his twenties, my
father, when they seized him and threw him into the ship that travelled
from Mesopotamia to Rome, and then from Rome to England, and to
South Shields.

One afternoon I left the Swallow George Hotel and walked over to the
bridge at Chollerford. I stood on the bridge remembering my ancestors
and I, who had not spoken Assyrian for 30 years, found myself
composing a song in my Assyrian/Aramaic mother tongue.

← *South Shields – South Pier, River Tyne entrance*
Photo: Steve Chettle

ܐܝܟ ܚܕ ܓܘܕܐ ܒܢܘܦܫܗ

***

ܡܚܝܠܝ ܝܡܝ ܡܚܝܠܝ
ܡܢ ܕܘܢܝܐ ܕܢܘܟܪܝܘܬܐ ܡܚܝܠܝ
ܠܐ ܝܕܥܢ ܩܡܘܕܝ ܕܘܢܝܐ ܝܠܗ ܢܘܟܪܝܘܬܐ . ܩܡܘܕܝ؟
ܐܝܟ ܚܕ ܐܢܫܐ ܗܘܠܝܠܗ ܠܓܢܗ. ܐܝܟ ܚܕ ܓܘܕܐ ܒܢܘܦܫܗ
ܝܠܗ ܒܪܘܢܟܝ ܝܡܝ
ܝܡܝ ܚܠܦܟܝ ܗܘܝܢ
ܐܡܘܪ ܩܐ ܒܒܝ:
ܣܢܩܐ ܠܐ ܟܪܝܗ ـ ܣܢܩܐ ܠܐ ܗܫܝܢܝܗ
ܒܪܘܢܘܟ ܟܝܒܠܘܟ ܟܝܒܠܘܟ
ܒܪܘܢܘܟ ܝܠܗ ܗܠ ܙܥܘܪܐ ܘܠܒܘܬܐ ܘܠܒܐ
ܠܒܗ ܝܠܗ ܪܒܐ ܓܘܕܐ
ܐܡܪܐ ܕܒܪܘܢܘܟ ܝܠܗ ܘܠܒܐ
ܣܢܩܐ ܠܐ ܟܪܝܗ ـ ܣܢܩܐ ܠܐ ܗܫܝܢܝܗ
ܡܚܝܠܝ ܝܡܝ ܡܚܝܠܝ
ܡܢ ܕܘܢܝܐ ܕܢܘܟܪܝܘܬܐ ܡܚܝܠܝ

Like a Lonely Wall

I am tired, O Mother. I am tired
of this strange world, I am tired.
I wonder why this world is so strange
Why?

Like a man who lost himself
like a lonely wall
who is your son, O Mother

Mother, I'd die for you
Tell my father
your boy is still young,
but his heart is bigger than his country

Kika, there's no need to be sad
no need to worry
Your son loves you

I am tired, O Mother, I am tired
of this strange world, I am tired
like a lonely wall
who is your son, O Mother

5

My father started working as a cook for the ferrymen and the slaves who worked at the mouth of the Tyne. One day a Roman guard discovered that they were all eating some strange little pastry things he hadn't seen before. 'They're called *claicha*,' the men told him. He ate one and found it very delicious. 'Where did you get them from?' he asked, and the ferrymen pointed to the deaf-dumb skinny man, who smiled back, held up his index finger and put it into a fist of his other hand. The Roman guard did not understand the gesture, but later that day, he took Kika to Arbeia Fort to make *claicha* for the soldiers and guards. How did Kika make *claicha*? Very easily, like this:

Claicha are simply little pastries made with dates. Take some dates and stone them. Then make dough from wheat flour and oil or butter, some sugar or honey, a little powdered fennel, a pinch of salt, and a little milk. Take a small piece of dough and roll it into a ball. Make a finger hole in it and put in a date. Close it up, and place on a tray. Put the date balls in a hot oven for ten minutes – until golden brown.

So now the Romans knew why this young cook was so popular with the ferrymen – he was cooking their own favourite food from back home. One of the Generals told Kika to make food for him too. He was taken to a big kitchen with large pantries and all the supplies he could need. However, he remained there a whole day without doing anything. The General brought one of the ferrymen over to talk with Kika and explain that he wanted Kika to be his cook and make meals for him. Kika smiled and nodded.

He took a full bucket of wheat to the miller who crushed it. Back in the kitchens he set about making *burghul kubba* and next day surprised the General with 10 *kubbas*. This is how he made them:

First, the burghul dough. Burghul are kernels of wheat that have been steamed, dried and crushed, and have been a staple food in Kika's part of the world since 5,000 BC, and some say 6,000 BC. After the dough, make the spicy, tasty filling.

Use two measures of burghul, one of farina, salt and black pepper, and mix together with some water. Leave for 45 minutes to let the water soak thoroughly into the burghul.

The filling needs two onions, chopped up finely, lamb cut up very small or minced, salt, black pepper, cumin, coriander, and some sliced almonds, all cooked together.

Press or roll out half the dough into the shape of a plate, put the cooked filling onto the dough, leaving a clear edge all round. Press or roll out the other half of the dough into another plate shape and place it over the first one with the meat filling inside. Press the two edges firmly together. Then cook it in a pan of boiling water for about ten minutes. When it is ready, lift it out carefully so that it doesn't break.

One day Kika saw the Romans eating roast chickens, so he decided the next dish to cook had to be *Tashreeb Dijaaj*.

For this spicy stew take some chicken, onion, garlic cloves, salt, noomi Basra (dried limes), coriander, curry powder and some chickpeas, a couple of hard-boiled eggs halved, and some flat bread like pittas.

Skin and clean a whole chicken and cut it into chunks. Peel the onions and cut them into chunks too. Skin a few garlic cloves. Put everything except the eggs into a large pot. Fill the pot half full with water, and when it is boiling skim off the froth. Then let it cook slowly until the chicken is very tender. Add the eggs when it is nearly done. The liquid of the stew should be very tasty, like a thick soup or broth.

Now comes the Tashreeb part. Get a large shallow dish, tear the pitta bread into pieces and place on the bottom of the dish. Pour the chicken stew over the bread and let it soak in. Now it's ready to eat.

Kika became a renowned cook among the Romans, and he stayed with them for years cooking Mesopotamian food. But from time to time he would make strange gestures: he would stroke both cheeks with his hands, point to his breasts with his index fingers, rub both fingers together and point into the distance. How he missed the woman he loved that he had left behind. But it seems nobody understood his gestures and nobody cared to understand. The selfish Romans thought only of their stomachs.

6

I am sitting in the train from Newcastle to London, thinking about the deaf-dumb cook who spent the rest of his life cooking for the Romans. I can hear him singing to his love:

Manny merreh leh bayennakh
Manny merreh bit shokinnakh
Atin khayey
Atin Khubby

Who said I don't want you?
Who said I abandoned you?
You are my life.
You are my love.

The renga

from Sea to Sea – renga days along Hadrian's Wall

The renga days provided some of the most public events connected to the Writing on the Wall project.

What is renga? It is a Japanese concept, meaning a collaborative, linked poem of twenty verses. But there is more to it than that. Certain rules must be followed and customs observed. A group of people join together for a day, gathered on a special portable platform equipped with sunshades and cushions, drinking green tea poured from a metal pot. The poem takes shape under the guidance of a master, helped by a host.

Under the direction of poet and artist Alec Finlay, eight renga days took place along the line of the Wall during September of 2003 and 2004, and each day produced a poem. The renga day encourages participants to think and to dream; to respond to the seasons and to the landscape. Finlay describes renga as 'oral and temporal before it becomes poems and print – the verses are so many notes for thoughts and feelings that pass between us over a day, as we share an experience of mood and strangers and friends connect'.

When the renga platform was erected at Heavenfield near Chollerford for the day, poet Linda France wrote, 'working with renga, it occurs to you, it's not by hand you write but by breath, coming and going, open as the sky above Heavenfield'.

From Arbeia to Bowness-on-Solway, renga spun a thread of poetry from east to west, bringing people together to share a unique experience.

Jacob Polley. Photo: Steve Chettle   *Photos: Morven Gregor (MG) Steve Chettle (SC)* →

Arbeia (MG)

→ *Walbottle (SC)*

→ *Walbottle (MG)*

→ *Housesteads (SC)*

→ *Housesteads (MG)*

Housesteads (MG)

→ *Heavenfield (MG)*

→ *Heavenfield (MG)*

→ *Heavenfield (MG)*

→ *Sandysike (SC)*

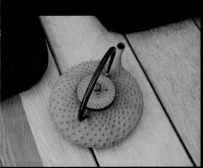

Sandysike (SC)

→ *Kirkandrews-on-Eden (SC)*

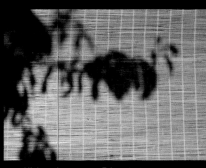

→ *Kirkandrews-on-Eden (SC)*

→ *Kirkandrews-on-Eden (SC)*

→ *Kirkandrews-on-Eden (MG)*

Bowness-on-Solway (SC)

→ *Bowness-on-Solway (SC)*

→ *Birdoswald (MG)*

→ *Birdoswald (MG)*

→ *Birdoswald (MG)*

Dove White

*(A nijuuin renga in summer
Arbeia, South Shields
3 September, 2003)*

Participants:

Steve Chettle
Alec Finlay (host)
Margaret Frayne
Morven Gregor
W. N. Herbert (master)
Miles Thurlow

Footnotes:

[1] *L. S. Lowry, the artist.*

[2] *Recreations of Roman wall paintings
depicting fruit trees and birds decorate the
Roman Villa at Arbeia.*

[3] *Soon hasty fame thro' the sad city bears /
[The mournful message to the mother's
ears.]; Dryden's translation.*

That gull could be a cloud,
Lowry[1], a legionary:
its wing refuses

over the sea the sky tilts
light falls slanting away

clear morning –
a slug draws slow
silver excretions on warming stone

dove white emulsion
protects from damp

its old roof removed
the fort is filling up with
air's blue granaries

painted pears wait[2]
for the afternoon sun

impatient hands –
conkers take their time
to fall

cargoes of people wave
sailing between the houses

at the corner shop:
The Chronicle, sausage rolls,
endangered fish

a post box swallows
the taste of the stamps

thin veneer scripts –
birthday guests
a line of Virgil

*interea pavidam volitans
pinnata per urbem*[3]

night's errata:
for shooting stars
read satellites

the little panes make ice cubes
out of the low sunless sky

fake snow
lying in drifts
deep into February

*sorry, I fell asleep –
my toes seem larger now*

hurrying to school
the mothers don't notice me
get out of their way

parked outside the Mithraic Temple
a pram wheel chariot

hungry now
the kids' egg sandwich:
anemone and celandine

making do
is the best of beauty.

Hadrian's Ghost

*(An eighteen-verse renga in summer
Walbottle Campus
5 September, 2003)*

Participants:

Jane Allen (Y11)
Jon Aydon (Y11)
Rebecca Boyd (Y13)
Lauren Bromley (Y11)
Ken Cockburn (master)
Leanne Conway (Y13)
Alec Finlay (host)
Morven Gregor
Kate Henderson (Y13)
Laura Hollocks (Y11)
Sheree Mack
Laura Steventon (Y11)
Miles Thurlow
Louise Wallbanks (Y11)
Hayley Wright (Y11)

Rosebay willow-herb –
summer's pink is loosening
to weightless white down

    spider lines muss the folds
    of your floppy sun hat

light cascades –
star circles rest
in the warm night

    twisted sheets
    at dawn

cold sweat –
leaves through the bars
carpet the concrete

    surge through stripped trees
    sink into mush

deception, deceit –
his devotion to coldness
deep as a ditch

    horse teeth, long tongue
    beauty of the bike shed

gleaming might
commands the river –
scenery slips by

    fixed to the wall
    a bald orange head

Hadrian's ghost
walks the line
protecting stones

    squares of light
    seep through the fog

compacted air
choking the dancers –
the beats throb

    is it his heart drumming
    through the church?

Easter
falls so late it bumps into
Mayday, the pagan

    forget-me-not
    forget-me-not

a year of dust –
the chintz endures
another spring clean

    the old woman
    drinks her tea.

Roman Holiday

*(A nijuuin renga in summer
Housesteads
7 September, 2003)*

Participants:

Alec Finlay (host)
Morven Gregor
Margaret Hall
Irene Leake
Gerry Loose (master)
Sadie Pape
Pauline Plummer
Ruth Sheldon
Miles Thurlow
Louise Wellington
Ezekiel Williams

Footnote:
[1] *A complete Roman latrine at Housesteads.*

Mint at the wall base –
all that's left
of legions' dreams

    the cat stretches
    in the middle of the path

patting a butterball
across
the afternoon sky

    moss blurs green
    angles of walls

bare fields
patterns of facts –
trigonometry

    spiders shelter
    trees begin to blaze

set the kindling
your way –
let's eat

    hot soup in bowls,
    grandma talks and talks

a blaring sound
in the distance
the morgue gets another

    from her to him
    just a glance

buckets of laughter
echo
from the latrines[1]

    bacon and sausage
    tea bags and legs

this one's tagged
FINAL DEMAND
for this quarter

    a shiver –
    all accounts are empty

paper and ribbon
tangle
in the pine

    no kite ever unscrambled
    its own lines

spare change chinks
in the bottle –
who will I holiday with this year?

    waking is easier
    in the earlier dawns

the blossom on that tree
been there for ages –
where am I?

    we walk further
    gather nettles and sorrel.

Background photo: Morven Gregor

Inset photos: Steve Chettle

Cloth Wings

*(A nijuuin renga in summer
Heavenfield
9 September, 2003)*

Participants:

Steve Chettle
Alec Finlay (host)
Linda France (master)
Margaret Frayne
Morven Gregor
Irene Leake
Sylvia Lynch
Aileen McKay
Lesley Mountain
Sadie Pape
Anne Race
Jadzia Race
Eileen Ridley
Miles Thurlow

Footnotes:

[1] *Heavenfield: site of battle between Oswald
of Northumbria and Cadwalla
of Gwynedd in AD 635.*

[2] *The Saint's bones were ascribed miraculous
powers of healing and led to
a cult of St Oswald spreading throughout
Europe during the Middle Ages.*

Another blue sky
shaking itself free
of swifts

   leaf shades
   on bamboo

a wind
from beyond
the moon

   secrets pass
   between the yew trees

branches crack underfoot
a phone rings –
where are my shoes?

   if it's a bear play dead
   for a lion fight back

she wakes
to tawny light
spilled on her pillow

   a blanket laid over
   the field of battle[1]

Vs in the mud –
the wall's not Roman
anymore

   at the edge of the forest
   a vixen seeks a mate

the stirrup cup
lathered flanks,
saddle sore

   soap bubbles squeeze
   from the sponge in your hand

butterfly cakes
bowl licked clean –
happy kids

   cloth wings hang
   in the cupboard

scratching a spy hole
on the frozen pane
I see a fire

   why do you keep on
   telling me fairy tales?

St Oswald's bones,[2]
a candle burning
through the afternoon

   sunlight bends and flexes
   a hare's hind legs

purple shadows
yellow coltsfoot
could shift tarmac

   kestrel silhouette
   moves away.

Talking on the Lawn

*(A nijuuin renga in autumn
Dharmavastu, Sandysike
6 September, 2004)*

Participants:

*Steve Chettle
Penny Dunbabin
Alec Finlay (master)
Morven Gregor
Irene Leake
Sara Lurati
Beth Rowson (co-ordinator)
Subhadassi (host)*

Footnotes:

[1] *Sandysike is surrounded by high chestnuts;
old apple trees grow in the garden.*

[2] *A stone circle near Penrith, Cumbria.*

[3] *The watermill at Little Salkeld, down the
road from Long Meg.*

[4] *Seasonal Affective Disorder.*

Alone with that old conker[1]
the one thing you'd miss
is an enemy

    cut stone laid heavy and high
    sour Bramleys, garden moons

breathe in damp air
listen to the silence
on the derelict frontier

    a cloud shrouded growl,
    what is its range?

turning left on the plane
lipstick smiles
greet each passenger

    he took his Powerbook everywhere
    even Halkidiki

a wall of heat
bleached umbrellas
jig on the sand

    gingerbread curls
    peel on the barge

a pebble skims
across
a superstition

    brush my hair at midnight
    waiting for a face

crossed fingers touch
an admiral
in the mirror

    knick of the blade
    tissue paper dab

bodily fluids, longings,
candle nub ends,
they recycle all they can

    snow angels
    on the lawn

for 4,000 years
Long Meg and Her Daughters[2]
haven't felt the cold

    the mill doors[3]
    open wide

smell of bread
pumped through
every supermarket

    the clocks go forward
    an end to S.A.D.[4]

billowing above the drive
gentians
on a linen pillowcase

    we've been talking all day
    on this hard bed.

The River Runs Backwards

*(A nijuuin renga in autumn
Kirkandrews-on-Eden
8 September, 2004)*

Participants:

Margaret Boumphrey

Steve Chettle

Alec Finlay (master)

Morven Gregor

Alan Hodgson

Stella Hodgson

Irene Leake

Sara Lurati

Jacob Polley (host)

Beth Rowson (co-ordinator)

Footnotes:

[1] *Chapelcross, the four towers of the nuclear
power station visible over the Solway Firth.*

[2] *The garrison along the wall included
auxiliaries from Morocco.*

Nettles and old docks
with liver spots,
inky brambles

> seedy teeth
> cobwebs muss my lips

Screech owl
cuts through
night's comfort

> barely awake
> but the sun says *make, make, make*

Chapelcross at full blast[1] –
the black melting road and wood
the light's broken into

> chalked silhouettes
> a flick of the line

tamped
the best Havana
scented air rolls out

> rum, lime and mint
> faded mojito bars

remember the hay barn?
I pulled the gold straws
from your hair

> in that pause
> she becomes another

glimpse of blue
her quick eyes
the river runs backwards

> a pair of herons
> angled dance

look
what the waterfall's
done to the moon

> jabbing at the crazed glaze
> the stamp surfaces

where is it from?
the magi follow
a black smudged star

> on the wall
> a Berber guards snow[2]

marked on the OS
every bridge
every pylon

> at Aballava's an orchard
> sheltered by ash

Judas ears
and ramsons sushi,
the perfect picnic

> tupperware lids
> not quite fitting.

Dog Coal

*(A nijuuin renga in autumn
Bowness-on-Solway
10 September, 2004)*

Participants:

*Denise Crellin
Alec Finlay (master)
Morven Gregor
Irene Leake
Martin Lucas (host)
Beth Rowson (co-ordinator)
Ann Ward*

Footnote:

[1] *A probe landed on the planet Mars
but failed to send back a signal.*

[2] *Trekkies, fans of the cult science
fiction series Star Trek.*

First low light
the bee loud glade
is electric

    swallows peg the lines
    with chatter

word is out
that the Perseids
are to fall

    the saltmarsh sifts
    flecks of iron

from the chain gang
there comes a song
of hate

    lost in the sun
    baked mud cracks

startled by spray
the lizard
forgets its tail

    a curling bookmark
    in between chapters

on the *Mountains of the Moon*
giant heathers
living obelisks

    the goat herd steps
    over our sleeping bag

it's a job to know
whose feet are these
bundled in knots

    a catafalque
    from Port of Valletta

that night
the mourners broke
all the windows

    each frozen puddle
    invites another jump

dog coal
spits and crackles
on the hooky mat

    toast with its own
    black holes

the Mars Probe[1]
signalling
nothing

    all the Trekkies[2]
    pull their ears

mares' tails
still belong
in this world

    . . . . swish
    stand up to the Firth.

Photos: Morven Gregor

The Walk Back

*(A nijuuin renga in autumn
Birdoswald
12 September, 2004)*

Participants:

Alec Finlay (master)
Morven Gregor
Irene Leake
David J. Platt (host)
Jacob Polley
Beth Rowson (co-ordinator)
Ruth Sheldon
Richard Thwaites

Footnotes:

[1] *Aretha Franklin.*

[2] *Spadeadam, site of the former Blue Streak
missile launching test programme.*

[3] *A carved phallus in the wall.*

[4] *Ardbeg, a malt whisky from Islay.*

[5] *Chough, a bird related to the crow.*

← renga at Housesteads and Sandysike

Crenelated stone
catches and holds
the wind

   spate rushes shale beds
   further down the river

silken leaves
circle
in moon pools

   I climb home
   over patchwork hills

at every other stile
there's a new Aretha[1]
to sing

   a ram's horns
   blue heat

streaks from Spadeadam[2]
have seared
through the woods

   a carved cock[3]
   points west

I'm first up
so loud around the house
while you sleep

   losing a day
   on the pillow's a note

wax orders,
ghosts tumble over
the landlocked bridge

   paint it white
   no one thought to ask

shut the door
when you're through
the room shakes with firelight

   Ardbeg passed[4]
   glass to glass

on the way back
the ice
meets itself

   boots crunch seaweed
   a chough glides into darkness[5]

dawn breaks another
sleepless night
raw edged with toothache

   early daredevils
   paddle the surf

offered flowers
and orange peel
washed ashore

   shoeless
   into the distance.

Host and master poets

from Sea to Sea – renga days along Hadrian's Wall was conceived by Alec Finlay who was the host poet in 2003 and master poet in 2004.

Each renga day was led by a master and host poet.

Poet	Location
W N Herbert	Arbeia
Ken Cockburn	Walbottle
Linda France	Heavenfield
Gerry Loose	Housesteads
David J Platt	Birdoswald
Subhadassi	Sandysike
Jacob Polley	Kirkandrews-on-Eden
Martin Lucas	Bowness-on-Solway

Some of these were also commissioned poets and their biographies are included in the main writers' section.

Morven Gregor was commissioned to photograph renga.

This project has been included in a book *Shared Writing: Renga Days* published by Platform Projects in 2005.

← *Birdoswald renga*
Photo: Steve Chettle

Photo: Morven Gregor

Alec Finlay

Alec Finlay is an artist, poet and publisher, who is currently artist-in-residence at the Yorkshire Sculpture Park. His recent exhibitions include *East 05* (Norwich Gallery) and *Avant-Garde English Landscape* (Yorkshire Sculpture Park). His recent publications include *turning toward living*, *Shared Writing*, *Ludwig Wittgenstein: There Were You Are Not*, *Mesostic herbarium*, *Wind Blown Clouds*, and *DtArNaCcEe DmAuNsCiEc*, a collaboration with Andrew Hodson. The *bookscapes* series he publishes was preceded by the *pocketbooks* series (1999–2002) and the *small press* series (2002–05). Alec lives and works in Byker, Newcastle upon Tyne.

Ken Cockburn

Ken Cockburn is a freelance poet, editor, translator and teacher. A former Assistant Director at the Scottish Poetry Library, he co-edited for the SPL the audio CD *The Jewel Box: Contemporary Scottish Poems* and *Intimate Expanses: XXV Scottish Poems 1978–2002*. With Alec Finlay he established and ran *pocketbooks*, an award-winning series of books of poetry and visual art (1999–2002). His poems are collected in *Souvenirs and Homelands*, which was shortlisted for a Saltire Award in 1998, and in many anthologies including *Dream State: The New Scottish Poets*. He is the editor of *The Dancers Inherit the Party: Early Stories, Plays & Poems* by Ian Hamilton Finlay.

Morven Gregor

Morven Gregor works as a photographer and theatre director. Her photographic work has appeared in various publications and publicity campaigns; including work for pocketbooks, platform projects, Rizzoli (New York), Latin American Bureau, *Island* magazine and the Hidden Garden. Her photographic philosophy is to celebrate the intimate and the overlooked, through the detail of human activity, such as making renga poetry. Current work includes images for Yorkshire Sculpture Park's Seed Catalogue and being one of the five photographers selected to represent Scotland in the Objective Nouvelle Vague in Brittany, 2006.

Gerry Loose

Gerry Loose is an award-winning poet whose works are as likely to appear in gardens or the landscape as in books. Informed on ecological and environmental principles, he works widely with a variety of community groups. He is Creative Director of the Peace Garden, and former Writing Fellow at Castlemilk, at the Botanic Gardens, Glasgow, and at Jardin des Plantes, Montpellier. His publications include *The Elementary Particles, a Measure* and *Tongues of Stone* as well as the forthcoming *Printed on Water: Selected & New Poems* and *Mouth of Silence*, a play for Birds of Paradise Theatre Company.

Photo: Steve Chettle

Photo: Martin Avery

Martin Lucas

Martin Lucas was born in 1962 in Middlesbrough and now lives in Preston. He has edited *Presence* haiku magazine since 1996 and is currently President of the British Haiku Society. In 2001 he completed a PhD on Haiku in Britain at Cardiff University of Wales. He co-edited *The Iron Book of British Haiku* (with David Cobb, 1998) and *The New Haiku* (with John Barlow, 2002).

David J Platt

David J Platt grew up and trained in the South of England but achieved escape velocity to Scotland by mid-'70s as a microbiologist/academic and stayed for 30 years. An interest in Eastern aesthetics began somewhere in the 80's, originally centred on ceramics and extended into haiku by the early 90's. Work published in a wide range of magazines and anthologies internationally, was awarded a Sasakawa Foundation prize in 2000 (Innovation in haiku studies) and a collection (Chasing Ripples) published 2001. Engineered early retirement in 2001, moved to Cumbria and set up a pottery.

Subhadassi

Subhadassi was born in Huddersfield in 1967. In 1992, he moved to the North East of England to establish the Newcastle Buddhist Centre. Whilst working there, his chapbook of poems *Sublunary Voodoo* was published by Mudfog. In 1998 he began to devote his time more fully to writing, and various commissions, residencies, grants and awards followed. His full-length poetry collection *peeled* was published by Arc in 2004, and its title poem received a special commendation in the 2005 Forward Prize. In 2006 he received an award from the Arts Council to work on his second full-length collection of poems. He currently lives in Northumberland.

Throckley performance →
Photo: Steve Chettle

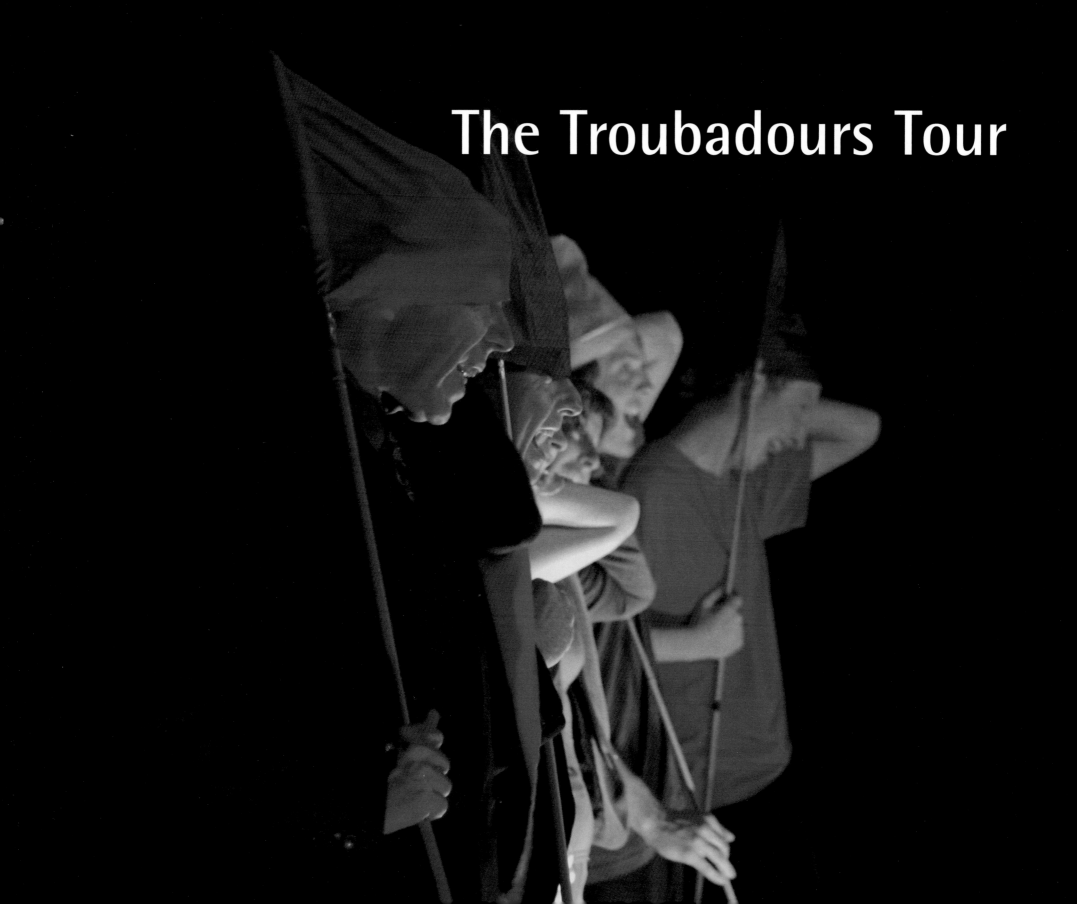

The Troubadours Tour

Walk the Wall

Cloud Nine – The Troubadours Tour

As the renga poets made a stately progress from east to west, The Troubadours were tramping sturdily from west to east. Flying colourful flags from their rucksacks, they were the only participants in the project who literally walked every inch of the Hadrian's Wall Path National Trail.

They brought a play written by Peter Mortimer and performed by his theatre company Cloud Nine, directed by Jackie Fielding. The theme of *Off the Wall* may seem bizarre, that the Wall could be bought by an aggressive businessman and turned into a profitable theme park, but Mortimer's comic satire steers alarmingly close to the truth at times. He raises important issues about how we should preserve, care for and engage with our historical and landscape treasures.

Although the eleven performances in village halls, pubs and forts along the Wall were at the heart of the tour, they formed the culmination of a creative programme at every venue. This involved schools, the WI, youth and community groups. Each venue designed and painted its own backdrop for the play, and the arrival of the actors on foot, as they would have done years ago, found an enthusiastic response from people who had been working on the project.

Peter Mortimer was very positive about bringing his play to the Wall, and felt that 'Hadrian's Wall had previously seemed the property of academics, historians, archaeologists and some actors walking about sporting Roman helmets and shields. *Off the Wall* was, we hope, an antidote to all that, and a bit of fun into the bargain. Let's face it, previously the Roman Wall has hardly ever been funny.'

Photos: Susie Burton (SB) Steve Chettle (SC) Stuart Firth (SF) Sara Lurati (SL)

← *Troubadours at Cuddy's Crags*
Photo: Sara Lurati/ARTS UK

Bowness-on-Solway *(SC)*

Low Crosby *(SL)*

Carlisle District *(SL)*

Walltown Crags (SC) →

Bowness-on-Solway performance (SC)

← *Dress rehearsal (SC)*

Walltown Crags *(SC)*

Hotbank Crags *(SL)*

Sycamore Gap *(SL)*

← *Throckley performance (SC)*

Newtown performance (SC)

← *Backdrop workshop, Newtown (SF)*

Steel Rigg (SC)

Marquee at Robin Hood Inn (SC)

Robin Hood Inn performance (SC)

Robin Hood Inn backdrop workshop at →
Queen Elizabeth High School, Hexham (SC)

Humshaugh performance (SC)

Heddon-on-the-Wall (SC)   *Newcastle Quayside (SB)*   *Segedunum, Wallsend*

← *Dilston College workshop (SC)*

Peter Mortimer

Peter Mortimer is a poet, playwright, editor and travel writer. His books include *Broke Through Britain*, about a 500 mile penniless trudge from Plymouth to Edinburgh; *100 Days on Holy Island*, recording a full winter spent on the remote North-East outpost; and his latest, *Cool for Qat: a Yemeni Journey*, which is linked to his play *Riot* about the 1930 Yemeni seamen's riots in South Shields. His book about the Roman Wall venture, *Off the Wall: The Journey of a Play*, will be published in 2006.

Off the Wall

Three extracts from his play

The play was performed and walked along Hadrian's Wall between 19–29 August 2004 at Bowness-on-Solway, Kirkandrews-on-Eden, Newtown, Gilsland, Twice Brewed, Humshaugh, East Wallhouses, Throckley and Wallsend, with two extra performances in North and South Shields on 30 & 31 August.

Characters *(in order of appearance)*

Modern Day

Drysdale	(A small businessman)	Dylan Mortimer
Loot	(A large businessman)	Dave Hollingworth
Cogno	(Loot's adviser)	Bill E. Meeks
Dolores	(Loot's wife)	Janine Birkett
Minister	(Govt. Minister for the North)	Alex Kinsey
Starlet	(A hedonistic young female)	Susie Burton

Roman Britain

Guard/Jailer	(Roman Guard)	Bill E. Meeks
Briginus	(Caledonian rebel leader)	Dave Hollingworth
Prisoner	(A Caledonian prisoner)	Dylan Mortimer
Ulpius Marcellus	(Roman Governor of Britain)	Alex Kinsey
Cingetissa	(Briginus' wife)	Janine Birkett

Several small parts played by members of the cast

Location:	The play is set both in modern and Roman Britain
Time:	21st and 2nd centuries AD

The millionaire entrepreneur Lionel Loot first explains to his unimpressed wife Dolores his plan to buy the Roman Wall.

Loot	All I ask is some respect!
Dolores	Respect?
Loot	I give you everything. You spit in my face.
Dolores	Where is the man I married? The real man?
Loot	The little man. The man of no consequence.
Cogno	Let me clean you up a bit sir. (STARTS)
Loot	Clean her up! Make her see sense!
Dolores	Was there anything else?
Loot	There was something else Dolores, yes. Who owns the Roman Wall, now?
Dolores	What is all this about the Roman Wall?
Loot	I repeat, who owns the Wall now?
Dolores	Very well. Various farmers and landowners. It is under the protection of English Heritage and is managed on behalf of the people.
Loot	Ah, the people. Does it make money?

Dolores	Thousands flock to see it every year of course, but –
Loot	(TO AUDIENCE) Is that what I asked her, whether thousands flocked to see it every year? Well? Course not. I asked her what – yes, that's right. Does it make money? Maybe Cogno knows the answer to this simple question.
Cogno	Income generation is not the Roman Wall's forte, as far as I know sir.
Loot	So. By most definitions, the Wall is a failure. I want to buy it.
Cogno	Buy it sir?
Dolores	Did you say – buy it?
Loot	No, I said there's a walrus eating the inside of my bottom. Yes, buy it, damn you!
Cogno	You want to buy the Roman Wall?
Loot	I'm in the nation of the deaf, the land of the failed hearing aid. I am among people whose ears contain more wax than a 20ft long candle. Yes – buy it!!
Cogno	But why would you want to buy the Roman Wall?
Loot	Why?
Dolores	You hate old things. You hate anything that has a history.

Loot	History is irrelevant.
Dolores	So why buy the Wall?
Loot	Why? Why? Why? Because – because... (PAUSE) I'll tell you why because. Then you'll see. Imagine this. An 80 mile long –
Dolores	That's Roman miles by the way. By our measurements it is only 73 miles.
Loot	I repeat, an 80 Roman miles long theme park. Customers get to travel the entire original length of the Roman Wall via mono-rail which is sealed in a transparent, weather-proof plastic tunnel.
Cogno	Inspired thinking sir.
Loot	There are video screens, holograms, actors dressed as Roman soldiers and barbarians.
Cogno	I see it even as you speak!
Loot	There are mock battles – an entire full day's travel and adventure without the need to leave your seat.
Cogno	Perfection almost.
Loot	I picture it now! Lionel Loot's Roman Wall Experience. Well?
Dolores	It stinks.

*Throckley performance 'Lionel Loot →
reveals his plan to buy Hadrian's Wall' (SC)*

Lionel Loot welcomes his prestigious guests and declares his newly acquired Roman Wall Experience open.

Loot   I give them what they want Cogno, even before they know they want it. That is why I am me, and they are they. Let the construction of the Roman Wall Experience begin! Build the perspex weather-proof tunnel!

(ALL THE FOLLOWING ARE ANIMATED)

Loot   Assemble and secure the 80 mile long mono-rail system. Install the one dozen giant touch button information screens! Activate the Roman centurion holograms! Complete conversion of 12 milecastles to pizza and burger bars! Choreograph and synchronize the warring Picts and Scots armies! The small details Cogno, I leave to you. Have I missed anything?

Cogno   I believe the Lionel Loot Roman Wall Experience awaits the official opening.

Loot   The guest list?

Cogno   All in order. The PM will be there, Elton John, Charlie Boy, Posh and Becks, Jonathan Ross. The latest Big Brother winner.

Loot   Is the hospitality tent stocked with the finest smoked salmon and strawberries?

Cogno   It is.

Loot   The champagne?

Cogno   The Moët is ready to pop.

Loot   Hot air balloons?

Cogno   122 of them, to mark the year that construction of the Wall began, will rise at the given signal along the length of the Wall.

Loot   The Red Arrows?

Cogno   Flying in a direct line from Segedunum to Bowness, leaving a vapour trail of purple. The colour of Imperial Rome.

Loot   The Italian ambassador?

Cogno   Already in the hospitality tent and slightly drunk.

Lionel Loot meets the Minister.

Minister   The government is exceedingly pleased with The Lionel Loot Roman Wall Experience.

Loot   I'm sure. Especially as the theme park passes through two marginal constituencies.

Minister   All factors are relevant. At the end of the day, given a level playing field, we have rebuffed critics claiming we neglect the rural Northern economy. The Wall's success enables us to ringfence certain priorities, and assures a customer satisfaction level commensurate with expectations.

Loot   Customer?

Minister   Yes, customer.

Loot   You mean, the voters?

Minister   The party has found the use of consumerist terminology is in tune with market trends. You requested an audience Mr Loot?

Loot   In non-consumerist terminology, I would now like this government to remove all the restrictions as to how I make use of the Wall and surrounding land.

Minister   Lift all restrictions?

Loot   At least your hearing is – what? – commensurate with expectations.

Minister   But I don't understand.

Loot   Life is so complex, I agree. But listen, it's simple enough. The Wall is now mine. I should be allowed to do what I like with it.

Minister   We are talking here about an important historic monument.

Loot   And I have made this historic monument highly lucrative.

Minister   Agreed.

Loot   And can make it even more so.

Minister   More so? Perhaps you could elucidate.

Loot   Perhaps I could. Lift the restrictions and I guarantee the financial benefit to the government will be many many times what it is now. Your customers will be delighted. You could even cut taxes.

Minister   Cut taxes?

Loot   Quite a shock isn't it? Tax cuts for the better-off, of course.

Minister   I see.

Loot	Imagine. The PM need never again face the nightmare prospect of taxing the rich more than the poor.
Minister	Give me the main bullet points of your proposal.
Loot	Bullet points?
Minister	Points one, two, three etc.
Loot	Tax cuts, tax cuts, and tax cuts.
Minister	The Wall has always had special protection. What you are asking is highly unusual.
Loot	Imagine the beneficial headlines in the *Daily Mail*. The praise from *The Sun*. I am talking the greatest tax cuts in living memory.
Minister	But to lift all restrictions on the Roman Wall.
Loot	What do restrictions do – except restrict?
Minister	Yes. I see.
Loot	Restricted use of old stones, or £20 a month more in take-home pay.
Minister	£20 a month?
Loot	Like I say, tax cuts, tax cuts, and tax cuts.
Minister	Why not simply tell me these – expansion plans?
Loot	I am a businessman. Businessmen reveal their full plans only at the most opportune moment.
Minister	I can assure you of this government's full confidentiality.
Loot	I've seen their full confidentiality on the front of the tabloids. Well? I'm a busy man.
Minister	I shall see what I can do.

A total of 23 community based workshops were held in July and August. These involved a wide variety of groups and individuals including primary and secondary schools, WI, Special Needs, Craft and Youth Groups, Children of Asylum Seekers, Elderly Day Care Users, Out of School Club.

The workshop leaders were:
o Visual Arts – Stuart Firth, Richard Jardine, Karen MacDougall, Gilly Walton
o Writing – Jim Eldridge, Janni Howker, Valerie Laws, Peter Mortimer
o Drama – Janine Birkett, Jackie Fielding

Each performance started with music from locally based musicians. These were Sue Dunn, Ruth Lambert, Roger Oram, Henry Robson, The Solway Band and Derry Yelding.

Steve Chettle / ARTS UK

Steve Chettle trained as a fine artist at Portsmouth Polytechnic and was a founder member of Art Space Portsmouth and ASPEX Gallery. Moving to the north in 1983, he ran Northern Print, was Visual Arts Officer for Cleveland Arts and Public Art Officer for Cumbria County Council, before becoming freelance in 1995 and establishing ARTS UK in 2000, where he is Director and Senior Consultant.

In addition to *Writing on the Wall*, his projects include: *Cleveland Visual Arts Festival*; *Riverscape - International Drawing Residencies for the River Tees*; Andy Goldsworthy – *Sheepfolds*; *Skylines*; *Elements – Public Art in Skelmersdale*; *100 Island Poems* Poetry Tour; and many public art commissions in the north east, north west and London.

More information:
www.arts-uk.com

ARTS UK

Acknowledgements

Writing on the Wall is part of Hadrian's Wall Tourism Partnership's Enrichment and Enterprise Scheme, a five-year initiative funded by One NorthEast and other partners.

Hadrian's Wall Tourism Partnership is a public and private sector partnership developing sustainable Arts, Business, Education, Tourism and Transport around the Hadrian's Wall World Heritage Site.

Writing on the Wall is an ARTS UK originated project which it is delivering on behalf of the Partnership by working closely with other public, private, voluntary and independent agencies in a series of community-based residencies and workshops.

Writing on the Wall is grateful for the funding and support of the many organisations below, without which the project would not have been possible.

*Pupil from Heddon-on-the-Wall St Andrew's CE First School,
taking part in an outdoor reading of W. H. Auden's
'Hadrian's Wall – An Historical Survey'.*   Photo: Steve Chettle